THREE SISTERS

AROUND THE GREEK TABLE

Three Sisters
AROUND THE GREEK TABLE

Betty Bakopoulos
Eleni Bakopoulos
Samantha Bakopoulos

adelfes

www.3greeksisters.com

DEDICATED TO

Our doting parents
Our dashing husbands
Our darling children

Authors Betty Bakopoulos, Eleni Bakopoulos & Samantha Bakopoulos

Photography by Eleni Bakopoulos
Additional Photography by Samantha Bakopoulos

Published by Adelfes

Printed and bound in Canada

Printed by AMP Gestions Impressions

A Catalog record for this book is available from the Library of Congress
ISBN 978-0-9813405-0-0

FIRST EDITION 2009

Discover more at www.3greeksisters.com
Books may be purchased online

Contents

Three Sisters

Picture an old three-storey red brick home in Toronto's Greek town. Our immediate family lived on the second floor, our uncle, his wife and four children were on the main floor, and tenants took up residence on the remaining two levels. It was a busy, loud, and colourful place to grow up. Greek was our first language and while living on Toronto's Danforth, it seemed that everyone was just like we were—Greek that is; from the butcher to the baker, to the grocery store owner, and even our family doctor.

Our parents immigrated from the Peloponnesus region of Greece, from small villages high in the mountains around Kalamata—famous for its olives. They farmed on small terraced gardens along steep hillsides and grew walnuts, peanuts, sesame seeds, olives, figs, beans, cucumbers, peppers, onions, potatoes, eggplants, and zucchini. They raised sheep and goats and from their milk made yogurt, and feta and Mizithra cheeses. They grew grapes, made wine, and even made their own pasta. Their produce was sold at markets, and what they could afford to keep became the basis for their meals and the basis of many of the recipes in this book.

Our father immigrated to Canada in the late sixties with much of his extended family. In order to join him our mother had to leave her entire family behind. Having no immediate family in Canada, she always longed for them and for Greece. Luckily for us, this meant several trips to Greece to connect with the other half of our family; trips that shaped and influenced us immeasurably.

We spent extended periods of time with aunts, uncles, and grandparents in the summer months of our youth. When many of our peers were at summer camp, we were in our mother's Greek village, fetching water from an underground spring and loading it up on horseback or making egg noodles and spreading them out on white sheets to dry in the sun. We even roasted lamb on a spit by the Neda River, in a scene reminiscent of a Bacchanal. We also frolicked in the temple of Apollo, a short walk from our maternal grandfather's home, in the days before it was roped off and protected by archaeologists. These moments were otherworldly and priceless. Nowadays, the mere sound of Greek music playing and the scent of Greek food cooking have the ability to transport us back, putting a weight on our chests, and a lump in our throats.

In our everyday life in Canada, as adults running our own households, cooking traditional Greek meals and handling our food is a connection to our heritage, and a connection to nature. Good organic produce, fresh herbs, wine, cheese, and marinated olives, are staples in our kitchens. Despite hectic schedules as teachers, artists, wives and mothers, we never regret the effort it takes to make a good meal. In fact, cooking teaches our children to value what they put into their bodies, it is a form of artistic expression, and it mothers us all.

Around the Greek Table

We woke up everyday to the sound of our father making us breakfast and preparing our school lunches. We were welcomed back into our home by the warmth of our mother's home cooked meals. Our parents worked long, hard hours. Their work schedule left us alone from 4:30pm every night until 2:00am, when they would return home to find us asleep in our beds. In order for us to be able to eat together as a family, our dinner time was 3:45pm. Unconventional and a little early, but we made it work.

Around our dinner table we all looked into each other's faces and shared our day and our lives. We celebrated achievements both big and small. We knew when our parents were stressed or tired. They knew when we were having trouble with friends or schoolwork. The emotional status of our independent lives was revealed around our dinner table even when no one spoke a word. A small appetite can betray a smile.

Connections happen over meals. Taking one's place around the family dinner table is one of the most important rituals in our lives. It reminds us we belong somewhere—it tells us that we are loved. Eating a good meal is chance to pause, connect with loved ones and recharge.

We have written each of these pages as a legacy for our children. When their place at our table sits empty and they find themselves starting their own family, may this book comfort them with delicious food and fond memories. May they see only love around their own dinner table in each and every direction.

Going Greek

If you are not Greek, then going Greek in the kitchen will be easy, put on some tunes, discover the recipes in this book, and enjoy yourself. If you are of Greek descent or you find yourself marrying into a Greek family, this book will save you many frustrating attempts to learn how to cook your favourite Greek dishes from your relatives. If they are anything like our mother, they measure nothing. Their cooking is intuitive and done by sight. Our mother would often say, a handful of this or a few pinches of that. We spent many exhausting days watching her cook, noting everything she did and measuring her handfuls and pinches. Some days she would surprise us by throwing an ingredient into a dish that she had never mentioned before, only to shrug it off when we would accuse her of keeping secrets. In this book, we have done all of the work so that your attempts to impress and please in the Greek kitchen will be a success every time. Your only worry, outdoing your mom, or heaven forbid, your Greek mother in-law!

Tips for Success in the Greek Kitchen

Firstly, always cook with this in mind—food is not just a means for survival. Cooking and eating can be one of the most sensuous and enjoyable aspects of your day.

Never prepare a meal the first time for guests—perfect it first with some practice. Taste your food while you are preparing it, season when needed, and feel free to add other ingredients to make the dish more to your liking. Let your taste buds be your guide!

Remember that the recipe is a guideline only; cooking times will vary from stove to stove and oven to oven, so please check your food often while you are cooking it.

Buy the freshest produce possible, and always use good Greek extra-virgin olive oil for everything except when deep frying.

Above all, embrace the experience of cooking, enjoy your food, and do both with those you love.

A Note About Photography

The food in every photograph in this book was devoured within minutes of completing the photo shoot. No fancy studio lighting, no special effects to make the dish look better. Over a period of several months, in the comfort of our homes, we cooked, we took photographs, we ate, we cooked, we took photographs and we ate some more . . . .

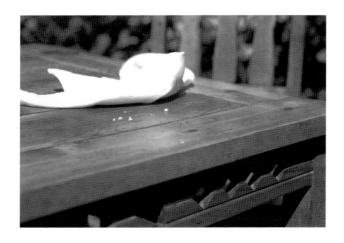

A Well-Stocked Kitchen

The typical Greek kitchen has the following food items on hand:

In the Pantry

Greek extra-virgin olive oil*
Vinegar, red wine, balsamic & white wine
Crushed tomato sauce
Tomato paste
Rice, Arborio
Lentils, brown
Kritharaki (Orzo)*
Chickpeas
Elephant beans*
Semolina*
Potatoes, yellow, white, baby red
Onions, yellow, white, red & Vidalia
Garlic
Honey
Walnuts
Sesame seeds
Dried figs
Confectioner's sugar
Ouzo*
Metaxa brandy*
Mavrodaphne*

In the Fridge

Feta cheese*
Kefalotiri cheese*
Mizithra cheese, finely grated*
Marinated Kalamata olives
Lemons
Oranges
Tomatoes
Cucumbers
Plain Yogurt, Greek or Balkan Style
Spinach
Eggplant
Zucchini
Capers
Anchovies
Fish Roe*

In the Freezer

Mizithra cheese, whole*
Greek sausage*
Greek coffee*
Meat sauce
Fresh parsley, basil and dill
washed & chopped, in
freezer bags

In the Herb Garden

Oregano
Thyme
Basil
Flat-leaf parsley
Spearmint

Off the Spice Rack

Sea salt, coarse & fine
Black Peppercorn
Oregano
Fennel, whole & ground
Cumin, whole & ground
Anise seed
Bay leaves
Cloves, whole & ground
Cinnamon, sticks & ground
Nutmeg
Ammonium bicarbonate
Mahlepi*
Mastiha*
Vanilla powder*

Item is defined in Glossary section

Breakfast is not often served in Greece. Most people have only a strong coffee to get their day going. Here in North America, we like to take the time to enjoy a good balanced breakfast.

This chapter is a collection of recipes that have become regular fare in our homes over the years. Most are a tribute to our dad, who enjoys making breakfast and always serves it with a proud face.

Breakfasts

Scrambled Eggs with Feta Cheese
Hard-Boiled Eggs with Lemon
Spinach & Feta Cheese Omelet
Greek Sausage with Orange Rind & Eggs
Leftover Lemon Chicken & Potatoes with Eggs
Warmed Yogurt with Honey, Ginger & Pistachios

Scrambled Eggs with Feta Cheese

Htipita Avya me Feta Tiri (Htee-pee-TAH Ahv-YAH meh FEH-tah Tee-REE)

If you like feta cheese you will love this dish. It is easy to prepare and delicious. Add as much feta as you like. For us, there can never be enough of it!

---

preparation 5 minutes   cooking 8 minutes   serves 2

---

2 tbsp olive oil
4 eggs
½ cup feta cheese, crumbled into large pieces

Heat the olive oil in a frying pan over high heat.

In a small bowl, whisk the eggs and stir in the feta cheese.

Add the feta and egg mixture to the frying pan and reduce the heat to medium. Use a spatula to scramble the eggs. Remove from the heat once the eggs are cooked through.

Serve immediately.

Hard-Boiled Eggs with Lemon

Vrazmena Avya me Lemoni (Vrahz-MEH-nah Ahv-YAH meh Leh-MOH-nee)

Our uncle made eggs this way for us when we were kids, and we loved them. It's a simple and unique way to freshen up the flavour of boiled eggs.

---

preparation 2 minutes   cooking 12 minutes   serves 2

---

4 eggs
4 lemon wedges
Salt
Pinch of paprika

VARIATION
Create an egg salad by mashing up the boiled eggs with a fork. The lemon juice will act as a binder instead of traditional egg salad with mayonnaise. This variation on egg salad is lighter and healthier.

Bring a small pot of water to a boil.

Place the eggs in the boiling water and boil for 12 minutes.

Remove the eggs from the water and run them under cold water. Peel and slice the eggs in half.

Squeeze lemon juice over the egg halves and top with some salt and paprika. Serve.

Spinach & Feta Cheese Omelet

Omeleta me Spanaki ke Feta (Oh-meh-LEH-tah meh Spah-NAH-kee keh FEH-tah)

Spinach and feta have a natural affinity for each other. Adding them to eggs makes for a perfect and healthy start to the day.

---

preparation 5 minutes   cooking 10 minutes   serves 1

¼ cup olive oil
1 shallot, minced
1 cup baby spinach, chopped
¼ tsp salt
¼ cup feta, crumbled
2 eggs

Heat 2 tablespoons of the olive oil in a frying pan over medium heat. Add the shallots and sauté until soft, about 3 minutes. Add the spinach and salt and cook until wilted. Remove from the heat, transfer to a bowl and add the feta cheese. Set aside.

In a small bowl, whisk the eggs.

Heat the remaining 2 tablespoons of olive oil in the same frying pan over high heat. Add the egg mixture to the frying pan and immediately stir the eggs with a fork once or twice. Allow the eggs to cook until lightly browned on the bottom side. Flip the omelet over with a spatula to cook the other side. Add the spinach mixture set aside earlier onto the centre of the omelet. Fold the omelet in thirds and remove from the heat once the eggs are cooked through.

Serve immediately.

Greek Sausage with Orange Rind & Eggs

Avya me Lokanika (Ahv-YAH meh Loh-KAH-nee-kah)

If you like sausage then seeking out Greek sausage with orange rind is well worth the effort. If you live in a large metropolis this shouldn't be too hard. The orange rind in Greek sausage offers an intense and unique flavour.

---

preparation 5 minutes   cooking 20 minutes   serves 4

¼ cup olive oil
1 Greek sausage
1 yellow onion, chopped
2 garlic cloves, pressed
6 eggs
¼ tsp each salt & pepper

VARIATION
Fried Greek sausage is flavourful and can be enjoyed on a party platter alongside salty cheeses such as kefalotiri or asiago.

Heat 2 tablespoons of the olive oil in a frying pan over medium-high heat. Add the sausage and cook until the sausage is brown and crispy on both sides. Transfer the sausage to a cutting board, slice and set aside.

In the same frying pan, heat the remaining olive oil over medium heat. Add the chopped onions. Sauté until soft, about 5 minutes.

Add the garlic and sauté for one minute.

In a small bowl, whisk the eggs, salt and pepper. Add the eggs and cooked sausage to the frying pan. Use a spatula to scramble the eggs. Remove from the heat once the eggs are cooked through.

Serve at once.

Leftover Lemon Chicken & Potatoes with Eggs

Kota me Patates ke Avya (KOH-tah meh Pah-TAH-tehs keh Ahv-YAH)

Chances that you will have leftover chicken and potatoes are slim, but if you do, then you can enjoy them with eggs. This dish was always our father's to make much to the satisfaction of our fiancés. Each one in their time would rave about this hearty and delicious breakfast while our Dad would smile proudly.

---

preparation 5 minutes   cooking 8 minutes   serves 4

---

2 tbsp olive oil
1 yellow onion, diced
2 garlic cloves, minced
2 cups leftover chicken and potatoes, cut into small pieces
4 eggs
¼ tsp each salt & pepper

LEFTOVERS
The recipe for *Lemon Chicken and Potatoes* can be found on page 167 and the leftovers can be used in this recipe.

Heat the olive oil in a frying pan over high heat.

Reduce the heat and add the diced onions. Sauté until soft, about 5 minutes.

Add the garlic and sauté for one minute.

Add the leftover chicken and potatoes. Heat through, about 2 minutes.

In a small bowl, whisk the eggs, salt and pepper.

Add the eggs to the frying pan. Use a spatula to scramble the eggs. Remove from the heat once the eggs are cooked through.

Serve.

Warmed Yogurt with Honey, Ginger & Pistachios

Yaourti me Meli (Yah-OOR-tee meh MEH-lee)

A delightful alternative to eggs in the morning, this breakfast is light and nourishing. Warmed yogurt and honey are a soulful base for spicy ginger and crunchy pistachios. Good morning!

preparation 3 minutes   cooking 2 minutes   serves 1

¾ cup yogurt, Greek or Balkan style
½-inch (12mm) fresh ginger, peeled, grated
Honey for drizzling
8-10 pistachios

Gently heat the yogurt and ginger in a small saucepan over medium heat. Remove from the heat once the yogurt is warmed through.

Transfer the yogurt and ginger to a serving bowl. Drizzle with honey and top with pistachios.

Serve warm.

Greeks love to socialize with food. Greeks love to drink with food.

In order to extend the socializing and drinking, much food is needed over many, many hours—hence the popularity of mezedes (appetizers).

Make enough of them and there is no need for a formal dinner at all!

Appetizers

Feta-Stuffed Phyllo Pastry Bites
Spanakopita
Baked Pumpkin or Zucchini Fritters
Parsley & Mint Meatballs
Spirit of Ouzo
Shrimp with Ouzo & Red Chilies
Saganaki
Grilled Octopus
Marinated Olives
Tsatziki
Stuffed Grape Leaves
Olive Tapenade & Goat Cheese on Pita Chips
Fried Calamari
Fish Roe Dip
Stuffed Sweet Peppers
Zucchini Ribbon Rolls
Santorini Croquettes
Zucchini Chips

Feta-Stuffed Phyllo Pastry Bites

Tiropites (Tee-ROH-pee-tehs)

Our relatives in Greece still make pastry with the basic ingredients of flour and water. On large tables, they spread the pastry paper-thin before filling it with a cheese stuffing. As you can imagine, making your own paper-thin pastry is time consuming and takes some practice, so we use frozen store-bought phyllo pastry instead. It tastes just as good as homemade pastry—just don't tell our aunts we told you so!

preparation 45 minutes	cooking 20 minutes	makes 36	bake 350°F (180°C)

2 cups feta cheese, crumbled
1 cup ricotta cheese
2 eggs, whole
2 egg yolks
1 cup unsalted butter
1 package phyllo pastry, thawed

MAKE AHEAD
Feta-Stuffed Phyllo Pastry Bites freeze really well. Place the triangles on a baking sheet lined with wax paper. Place the baking sheet in the freezer for 20 minutes. Remove and transfer the triangles to a freezer bag. Place waxed paper in between each layer and store in the freezer for up to 2 months. They can be cooked in the oven from frozen. *Feta-Stuffed Phyllo Pastry Bites* can also be made on the morning of serving day and refrigerated until ready to bake.

In a medium-sized bowl, add the feta cheese, ricotta cheese, and eggs. Mix with a wooden spoon until thoroughly combined. Set aside.

Melt the butter in a small saucepan over low heat. Remove from the heat and skim away any foam. Use only the clarified butter and avoid the milk solids that have settled at the bottom of the pan.

Remove the phyllo pastry from its package. Leaving it rolled up, use a sharp knife to divide the phyllo into 3-inch (7.5cm) segments. There will be a small strip of phyllo left over, just discard. Take the first segment of phyllo and roll it out onto a clean work surface. Leave the remaining phyllo rolled up and covered with a damp cloth to avoid drying out.

Take two individual phyllo sheets and use a pastry brush to lightly brush each sheet with some melted butter. Lay them on top of each other. Spoon 1 tablespoon of the cheese mixture at the narrow end of the phyllo. Lift up the phyllo at the narrow end and fold it over the filling. Lift the bottom right corner of the phyllo up and over to the top left. Take the bottom left of the phyllo and fold up and over to the top right. Your pastry should start to take the shape of a triangle. Repeat this folding pattern until you run out of pastry.

Lightly brush the top of the triangle with butter and place it on a parchment-paper lined baking sheet seam-side down.

Repeat this process with the remaining phyllo sheets and filling.

Place the triangles in the middle of a preheated oven and bake for 15-20 minutes until golden brown and flaky.

Serve warm.

See phyllo pastry tips on page 221.

Spanakopita

(Spah-nah-KOH-pee-tah)

Traditional spanakopita does not have feta cheese in it but our mom always made it with lots of feta. We have often been disappointed when we have ordered spanakopita in restaurants, forgetting that it is usually made in the traditional way. Spanakopita with or without feta—it is up to you!

preparation 30 minutes + 30 minutes refrigeration time   cooking 45 minutes   makes 6 pieces   bake 350°F (180°C)

2 tbsp olive oil
8 scallions, chopped, both white & green
2 bunches spinach, 2lb (1.25kg) tough ends removed & coarsely chopped
½ cup fresh parsley, chopped
¼ cup fresh basil, chopped
2 tbsp fresh dill, chopped
2 cups feta cheese, crumbled into large pieces
Pinch of salt
2 egg yolks
½ cup unsalted butter
10 sheets phyllo pastry, thawed

MAKE AHEAD
After 30 minutes refrigeration time, Spanakopita can be transferred to the freezer and kept frozen for up to 2 months. It can be cooked from frozen.

See phyllo pastry tips on page 221.

Place the olive oil in a large saucepan over medium heat. Add the scallions and cook for 2 minutes. Add the spinach and cook until wilted. Place the spinach and scallions in a colander. Press lightly with a wooden spoon to remove the excess water. Transfer to a bowl and combine with the parsley, basil, dill, crumbled feta, salt and egg yolks. This is the filling.

Melt the butter in a small saucepan over low heat. Remove from the heat and skim away any foam. Use only the clarified butter and avoid the white milk solids that have settled at the bottom of the pan.

Gather two of the phyllo sheets and cover the remaining sheets with a damp cloth to avoid drying out. Lay the two sheets of phyllo along the bottom of a 9x13-inch (33x23cm) shallow baking dish, and allow the sheets to slightly overlap in the center of the pan and the excess to hang over the sides of the pan. Brush these sheets lightly with some melted butter. Arrange another six sheets of phyllo in the same manner, brushing each sheet with melted butter. Spread the filling prepared earlier in an even layer on top of the pastry.

Gather the phyllo pastry hanging over the sides of the pan and fold over to enclose the spinach filling. Brush each layer with melted butter. Lay the remaining two layers of phyllo pastry on the very top and allow the phyllo to wrinkle and fold to create a ruffled top. Brush with melted butter. Cover in plastic wrap and refrigerate for 30 minutes.

Remove from the refrigerator and lightly sprinkle the top of the spanakopita with water. Place in the middle of a preheated oven and bake until golden brown and crispy, about 45 minutes. Cut into serving pieces and serve warm or cold.

VARIATIONS To prepare *Spanakopita* triangles follow the folding patterns for *Feta-Stuffed Phyllo Pastry Bites* on the previous page.

Baked Pumpkin or Zucchini Fritters

Kolokithopites (Koh-loh-kee-THOH-pee-tehs)

Zucchini grows in our parent's backyard every summer—a jungle of giant green leaves with large yellow flowers. The zucchini is fried, baked, stuffed and eaten relentlessly. Our favourite transformation of zucchini is our mom's baked fritters. In the fall, pumpkin fritters replace zucchini fritters, and are always on the table at Thanksgiving. We are thankful for that!

preparation 35 minutes   cooking 25 minutes   makes 16   bake 425°F (220°C)

1 small pumpkin or
3 small zucchini, about
1lb (500g), grated
½ tsp salt
2 potatoes, ½ lb (250g),
peeled
4 garlic cloves, minced
4 scallions, chopped,
both white & green
1 cup feta cheese,
crumbled
¼ cup fresh bread
crumbs
¼ cup each fresh mint &
basil, chopped
1 egg
Olive oil for greasing

MAKE AHEAD
The zucchini patties can be prepared and refrigerated on the morning of serving day until ready to bake.

Place the grated zucchini in a colander. Add the salt and set aside for 15 minutes. Squeeze the excess moisture from the zucchini with your hands and place in a medium-sized bowl.

Parboil the potatoes for 10 minutes in a large pot of boiling water. Drain and set aside to cool. Coarsely grate the parboiled potatoes over the bowl with the zucchini.

Add the remaining ingredients to the bowl and use your hands to mix the ingredients together.

Shape the zucchini mixture into patties and use a brush to lightly grease each side of the patty with olive oil. Place the patties on a baking sheet and place in the upper third of a preheated oven for 15 minutes until golden brown. Flip and bake for 10 minutes further. Serve warm.

TIP
Make your own bread crumbs for this recipe by placing a slice of bread in a food processor.

Parsley & Mint Meatballs

Keftedes (Kehf-TEH-dehs)

The use of fresh aromatic herbs make these meatballs super tasty. Kids love them as an easy finger food or added to tomato sauce and pasta. For adults—they are the perfect *meze* to be enjoyed with a strong spirit like Ouzo. They can also be served with a *Lemon, Oregano and Olive Oil Dressing and/or Tsatziki* for dipping.

---

preparation 10 minutes + 1 hour refrigeration time   cooking 20 minutes   makes 30 meatballs   bake 450°F (230°C)

1lb (500g) ground beef, extra lean
½ yellow onion, minced
½ cup each fresh parsley & mint, chopped
½ cup fresh bread crumbs
1 egg
1 tbsp yellow mustard
1 tbsp fresh lemon juice
1 tbsp oregano, dried
½ tsp salt
Pepper, as desired

Lemon, Oregano & Olive Oil Dressing recipe, see page 262.

Combine all of the ingredients in a large bowl and mix thoroughly with your hands. Let this mixture sit in the refrigerator for at least an hour.

Shape the meat into bite-sized balls and place on a lightly greased baking sheet.

Place in a preheated oven for 15-20 minutes until brown and cooked through.

Prepare the *Lemon, Oregano & Olive Oil Dressing*. Drizzle the sauce over the meatballs and serve warm or at room temperature.

TIP
Make your own bread crumbs for this recipe by placing two slices of bread in a food processor.

VARIATION
Turn the meatballs into burgers by creating larger patties. You can make about 12 patties with this recipe.

MAKE AHEAD
The mixture can stay in the refrigerator for 1 hour or up to 1 day in advance before being shaped into bite-sized balls.

The Spirit of Ouzo

Ouzo's anise flavour is very refreshing in the summer heat. It is often served with mezedes: various grilled meats, or seafood such as calamari and octopus.

Chill your bottle of ouzo and pour a shot into a highball glass filled with ice cubes. The ouzo will turn cloudy. You may add water to dilute the ouzo further if it is too intense. This is perfectly acceptable and is done quite regularly in Greece.

Ouzo is meant to be savoured. Sip it while enjoying some appetizers in the company of friends.

Shrimp with Ouzo & Red Chilies

Yarides me Ouzo (Yah-REE-des meh OO-zoh)

Ouzo's anise flavour pairs well with shrimp. The red chilies add a zing and the cream cheese finishes this appetizer off quite nicely. This simple shrimp recipe is ideal for entertaining.

---

preparation 10 minutes   cooking 10 minutes   serves 4

---

1 tbsp butter
1 tbsp olive oil
12 jumbo shrimp, 1lb (500g), peeled, deveined, patted dry
2 garlic cloves, minced
1 tsp red pepper flakes
⅛ tsp salt
¼ cup Ouzo
1 tsp cream cheese

Heat the butter and oil in a frying pan over high heat. Lay the shrimp flat in the pan. When the shrimp turn pink use tongs to flip them over.

Add the garlic, red pepper flakes and salt. Cook for 3 minutes while gently moving the ingredients around.

Add the Ouzo and cook until almost evaporated.

Mix in the cream cheese and remove the pan from the heat once the cheese has melted.

Arrange the shrimp on a serving platter and serve piping hot.

Saganaki

(Sah-gah-NAH-kee)

Bright beautiful flames, the smell of melting cheese, and the sound of a waiter yelling "Opa!" The senses come alive whenever saganaki is served. This impressive flambéed cheese dish, though intimidating, is actually quite simple to do and needn't be reserved for Greek restaurant outings.

---

preparation 5 minutes   cooking 5 minutes   serves 4

Kefalotiri cheese, cut into ¼-inch (6mm) thick slab
Flour for dusting
2 tbsp olive oil
2 tbsp Metaxa, or other brandy
2 lemon wedges

FLAMBÉEING
Whenever you flambé something ensure that you keep your hair and loose clothing tucked away. Also, keep a lid handy to smother the flame if it gets too high.

Rinse the kefalotiri slabs with water, lightly pat dry and dust with flour.

Heat the olive oil in a frying pan over high heat.

Place the slab of cheese in the hot oil until golden-brown on both sides, about 2 minutes per side.

Remove the pan from the heat. Pour the brandy on the hot cheese and immediately light the brandy with a match—be careful! Squeeze the lemon wedges on the cheese to help put the flames out.

Transfer to a serving platter and serve immediately. Opa!

SUBSTITUTIONS
Kefalograviera, Kasseri and feta cheeses can be used to make *Saganaki*.

Grilled Octopus

Ohtapodi Psito (Oh-htah-POH-dee Psee-TOH)

We have memories of our uncle in Greece repeatedly pounding a large octopus on the ground to tenderize it; apparently the magic number is 40 times. After it was tenderized it was hung up to dry in the scorching sun for at least a day. Any squeamishness we may have had at the thought of eating octopus disappeared with the first bite we ever took! Octopus is delicious and can be cooked in many different ways. Grilling and marinating octopus is the most common way to eat it in the summer. When buying octopus, be sure to ask your fishmonger for octopus that has already been tenderized.

---

preparation 10 minutes + overnight marinating   cooking 1 hour 10 minutes   serves 4

---

1 octopus, 3lbs (1.5kg)

FOR THE MARINADE
½ cup olive oil
1/3 cup red wine vinegar
1 tsp fresh oregano,
chopped
2 garlic cloves, pressed

Lemon wedges

Remove the head and beak from the octopus using a sharp knife, and discard. Rinse the octopus.

Place the octopus in a large pot and cover with water. Low-boil the octopus for 60 minutes, or until it is tender. Drain.

Cut the tentacles from the sac. Discard the sac and leave the tentacles whole. Place the tentacles in a glass bowl.

Prepare the marinade in a small bowl. Pour half of the marinade over the tentacles. Cover in plastic wrap and refrigerate overnight. Cover the remaining marinade with plastic wrap and refrigerate.

To serve the octopus, place the marinated tentacles on a preheated grill and cook over medium-high heat until slightly charred and crisp.

Transfer the octopus to a platter and drizzle with the reserved marinade. Serve with lemon wedges.

Marinated Olives

Elies (Eh-lee-EHS)

The sight of an old olive tree is arresting. The older they are, the more twisted and magnificent their shape becomes. They survive for hundreds of years in very hot and arid climates. Their will to keep on giving, generation after generation, makes this tree almost holy in Greece.
No matter the meal, Greek marinated olives will always find their way to the dinner table.

preparation overnight soaking time + 5 minutes

1 cup Kalamata olives
2/3 cup olive oil
3 tbsp red wine vinegar
2 tbsp balsamic vinegar
1 tbsp oregano, dried
1 tsp red pepper flakes
(optional)

MAKE AHEAD
We always have marinated olives in our refrigerator. They can last for several months.

Soak the olives in a bowl of fresh water overnight. This helps remove the salty brine that the olives come packed in. Drain.

Add the olives with all of the remaining ingredients to a favourite glass jar with a lid. Mix and refrigerate. The longer the olives marinate the better they taste.

Remove the olives from the refrigerator 30 minutes before serving so that the olive oil has time to liquefy again.

Bring marinated olives to the dinner table with just about any meal or save for a party platter.

Tsatziki

(Tsah-DZEE-kee)

Tsatziki is a staple in our homes. Tsatziki can accompany chicken, pork or lamb dishes. When you develop a real love for tsatziki (as we have) then you will want it with bread, pitas or even lemon potatoes!

---

preparation 15 minutes + 4 hours straining time   makes 1 cup

---

1 cup yogurt, Greek or Balkan style
½ cucumber, peeled & grated
2 garlic cloves, pressed
1 tbsp olive oil
1 tsp white wine vinegar
¼ tsp each salt & pepper
Pinch cayenne pepper
Parsley sprigs

BREATH FRESHENER
Eat a sprig of parsley after you've finished eating tsatziki. It's a great natural breath freshener!

Place a fine mesh strainer over a bowl. Add the yogurt and set aside in the refrigerator for 4 hours or overnight.

Transfer the strained yogurt to a serving bowl.

Squeeze the grated cucumber with your hands and remove the excess water. Add it to the yogurt.

Add the remaining ingredients to the yogurt and mix thoroughly.

Dust with some cayenne pepper and garnish with parsley sprigs.

Keep the yogurt and cucumber dip in the refrigerator until ready to serve.

Serve with pita wedges or alongside grilled or roasted meats.

MAKE AHEAD
Tsatziki can be made 2 days in advance. Keep in mind that the potency of the garlic in the tsatziki intensifies the longer it sits!

Around the Greek Table

Stuffed Grape Leaves

Dolmades (Dohl-MAH-dehs)

The quality of the grape leaves determines the success of this dish.   We pick the youngest grape leaves on our pergola and fill them with aromatic herbs and rice. They make a superb appetizer.

---

preparation 30 minutes   cooking 30 minutes   makes 40

---

50 grape leaves
1 cup Arborio rice
½ cup each fresh dill,
mint, parsley, chopped
5 scallions, chopped
both white & green
1 tsp salt
¼ cup olive oil
Pinch cayenne pepper
Pepper, as desired
Lemon wedges

GRAPE LEAVES
Grape leaves can be found jarred and preserved in water or vinegar brine. If you are lucky, they can also be found fresh on the vine in your own backyard!

Place the grape leaves in a large pot of boiling water and boil for 5 minutes until slightly softened. Strain. Set aside 10 grape leaves to line your pot and place the remaining grape leaves on a work surface.

Mix all of the other ingredients together in a medium-sized bowl. On a flat work surface, lay a grape leaf down, spiny-side up. Place one teaspoon of the filling at the bottom of the leaf closest to you. Roll the leaf up once, fold the sides of the leaf inwards and continue rolling away from you. The filling should be completely encased in the grape leaf. Set the stuffed grape leaf aside and repeat with the remaining leaves.

Line a wide-bottomed pot with five of the grape leaves set aside earlier. Place the stuffed grape leaves next, seam-side down and close together. Cover with the remaining 5 grape leaves. Pour in enough boiling water to just cover the leaves. Place a plate on top of the leaves to help hold the stuffed grape leaves down while cooking.

Bring to a boil, lower the heat and simmer until the rice is cooked through, at least 30 minutes. Serve warm or cold with lemon wedges.

SUBSTITUTIONS
Grape leaves can be substituted with collard greens. You will need to cut away the hard spine of the leaf before blanching it and stuffing.

VARIATIONS
Add ½ cup ground beef or veal, plus ½ tsp more salt to the mixture for a change.
Add ½ cup walnuts and raisins to the mixture.
Top with *Lemon and Egg Sauce*, see page 260, to serve as a vegetarian entrée or side dish.

Olive Tapenade & Goat Cheese on Pita Chips

Spasti Elia se Pita (Spahs-TEE Eh-lee-AH seh PEE-tah)

In our humble opinion, this is the best tapenade recipe out there!

---

preparation 10 minutes   cooking 10 minutes   makes 1 cup   bake 400°F (200°C)

---

1 cup Kalamata olives
¼ cup capers
4 garlic cloves, whole
4 preserved anchovy fillets, rinsed
½ cup fresh basil
¼ cup olive oil
2 tbsp fresh lemon juice
1 tsp Metaxa, or other brandy, (optional)
2 Greek-style pitas
Olive oil for coating
Goat cheese

MAKE AHEAD
Transfer the *Olive Tapenade* to a glass jar with a lid and store in the refrigerator for up to 2 weeks.

Smash the olives with a mallet, remove the exposed pit by hand and discard. Place the pitted olives in a food processor.

Add the capers, garlic, anchovies, basil, olive oil and lemon juice to the food processor and process until slightly chunky.

Stir in the Metaxa or other brandy if desired.

To prepare the pita chips, cut a 6-inch pita into 8 wedges. Use a brush to lightly coat the pita wedges with olive oil. Transfer to a baking sheet and bake in a preheated oven for 5 minutes, flip and bake 5 minutes further or until golden and crisp. Remove from the oven and transfer to a serving platter.

Spread some goat cheese on each pita chip and top with a scoop of the olive tapenade. Serve.

VARIATION
Olive Tapenade can also be served alongside a grilled steak.

Fried Calamari

Calamarakia (Kah-lah-mah-RAH-kee-ah)

Calamari is an essential meze in the summertime; perfect with a nice cold beer and a good group of friends. In our family, we always have to make a batch just for the kids, because they love their calamari! Serve hot with lemon and *Tsatziki* dip.

preparation 10 minutes   cook 2-3 minutes per batch   serves 4

2 lb (1kg) calamari, cleaned & sliced into ¼-inch (6mm) rings
1 cup all-purpose flour
2 tbsp cornstarch
1 tsp salt
1 tsp parsley, dried
Vegetable oil for frying
Lemon wedges

Tsatziki dip, see recipe page 53

MAKE AHEAD
Calamari can be cleaned and sliced into rings on the morning of serving day and kept in the refrigerator until ready to fry.

USING A THERMOMETER
If you're using an oil thermometer, let the oil reach 350°F (180°C) before placing the calamari in the oil.

Remove any excess water from the calamari using a paper towel.

Mix the flour, cornstarch, salt and parsley together in a medium-sized bowl.

Fill a large heavy saucepan with oil to a depth of 3-inches (7.5 cm). Heat the oil over high heat. Coat the calamari in the flour mixture and shake off the excess. Working in batches, place the calamari in the frying pan with the hot oil. Fry for 2 minutes. Remove the calamari with a slotted spoon and transfer to a platter lined with paper towel. Repeat with the remaining calamari rings.

Place the calamari on a serving platter and squeeze lemon juice over the fried calamari. Serve at once with *Tsatziki* for dipping.

CLEANING CALAMARI
You can buy bags of frozen calamari that have already been cleaned and cut into rings; or you can buy whole calamari and prepare them yourself. To prepare the calamari, you will need to pull the tentacles away from the body. Clean out the inside of the body and pull out the thin clear cartilage that runs along the inside. Rinse the calamari thoroughly under cold water. If the calamari has a spotted membrane, pull it off and discard. Use a sharp knife to cut the calamari into rings. If using the tentacles, cut the tentacles away from the head just below the eyes. Squeeze the tentacles to remove the hard round "beak" at the base. Discard the head and beak and rinse the tentacles. Repeat this process with the remaining calamari.

Fish Roe Dip

Taramosalata (Tah-rah-moh-sah-LAH-tah)

This dip will range in colour from light peach to bright pink according to the roe used. Growing up, we would often refer to it as the "poor man's caviar". It has a salty taste that makes it a great appetizer with drinks. Serve it with crunchy pita chips, or bread sticks.

---

preparation 10 minutes + 30 minutes refrigeration time   makes 2 cups

4 slices white bread, crusts removed
3 potatoes, about 600g, peeled & boiled
4oz (115g) roe of carp, codfish, lumpfish or grey mullet
1 yellow onion, minced
½ cup olive oil
Juice of 2 lemons

MAKE AHEAD
The *Fish Roe Dip* can be stored in an airtight container and refrigerated for up to 2 days before serving.

Place the bread in a bowl of water and soak for 5 minutes. Remove the bread and squeeze the excess water. Place in a food processor.

Add the potatoes, roe and onion to the food processor and purée. Once the ingredients are combined, continue to process the dip while slowly pouring in the olive oil followed by the lemon juice.

Transfer the dip to an airtight container, let it cool and refrigerate for at least 30 minutes before serving.

Stuffed Sweet Peppers

Ylikes Yemistes Piperies (Ylee-KEHS Yeh-mee-STEHS Pee-peh-ree-EHS)

Warm, melted, creamy cheese stuffed inside roasted peppers makes for a sweet and salty treat. This super tasty starter also pairs well with fish and meat as part of a main entrée.

---

preparation 10 minutes   cooking 10 minutes   serves 4   broil 500°F (260°C)

---

6 sweet cubanelle peppers
1 ½ cups feta cheese, crumbled
½ cup ricotta cheese
¼ cup each fresh basil & oregano, chopped
¼ cup olive oil
2 tbsp semolina
¼ tsp sweet paprika
⅛ tsp cayenne pepper

MAKE AHEAD
The stuffing mixture can be prepared on the morning of serving day and refrigerated until ready to use.

Cut the ends off the peppers and seed them. Set aside.

In a small bowl, add the remaining ingredients and mix with a wooden spoon until thoroughly combined.

Using a spoon, stuff the peppers with the mixture and lay the peppers flat on a baking sheet. Do not overstuff the peppers.

Place the baking sheet in the upper third of a preheated oven and broil for 3-5 minutes on each side. Transfer to a serving platter. Serve warm.

VARIATION
Use hot banana peppers instead for a spicy change or try Jalapeño peppers for a Greek version of a Jalapeño popper.

Zucchini Ribbon Rolls

Kolokithi se Rolaki (Koh-loh-KEE-thee seh Roh-LAH-kee)

Our kids refer to this appetizer as "Greek sushi". It looks beautiful on an appetizer platter and tastes even better!

---

preparation 20 minutes   cooking 5 minutes   makes 20 ribbon rolls

---

4 zucchini, sliced
lengthwise, ¼-inch
(6mm) thick
Olive oil for coating
Salt
½ cup goat cheese
2 garlic cloves, pressed
¼ cup sun-dried
tomatoes
5 fresh mint leaves,
chopped
Chives for tying

Brush the zucchini slices with olive oil and sprinkle with salt.

Lay on a preheated grill and grill for 2 minutes on both sides. Set aside.

Combine the goat cheese, garlic, sun-dried tomatoes and mint in a small bowl.

Lay the zucchini slices on a flat work surface and spread a thin layer of the goat cheese mixture over the entire surface of the zucchini slice. Roll the zucchini up and tie with a chive. Repeat with the remaining zucchini slices.

Arrange on a serving platter and serve.

MAKE AHEAD
Zucchini Ribbon Rolls can be prepared and refrigerated up to 3 hours in advance.

WORKING WITH CHIVES
Drop the chives in a pot of boiling water. Immediately remove and transfer to a cold water bath; this will help prevent the chives from breaking when they are being used as ties.

Santorini Croquettes

Domatokeftedes (Doh-mah-toh-kehf-TEH-dehs)

We first tried these croquettes in Santorini, where they are a specialty proudly served in taverns throughout the island. They are absolutely mouthwatering. Like many fried appetizers, they need to be served piping hot and crispy!

---

preparation 20 minutes   cooking 6 minutes per batch   makes 12 croquettes

---

3 tomatoes, chopped
6 scallions, chopped
both white & green
2 garlic cloves, minced
¼ cup fresh mint and
basil chopped
1 tbsp baking powder
½ tsp salt
2/3 cup all-purpose flour,
plus 1/3 cup reserve
Vegetable oil for frying

Mix the tomatoes, scallions, garlic and herbs together in a medium-sized bowl with your hands. Add the baking powder, salt and flour. If the mixture is too runny add up to 1/3 cup more flour.

Gather a small handful of the mixture into your hands and pack it tightly into a ball. Flatten slightly and set aside. Repeat with the remaining mixture.

Pour enough vegetable oil into a wide-bottomed skillet to create a depth of 2-inches (5 cm). Heat the oil over high heat.

Place the croquettes into the hot oil and cook until golden-brown on both sides, about 3 minutes per side. Remove from the oil and arrange on a plate lined with paper towel to absorb the excess oil.

Transfer to a serving platter and serve while hot.

Zucchini Chips

Tiyanita Kolokithia (Tee-yah-nee-TAH Koh-loh-KEE-thee-ah)

Our mom made these zucchini chips for us when we were young and we thought they were the coolest snack. We discovered them again as adults at high-end Greek restaurants and realized we were pretty lucky kids!

---

preparation 20 minutes   cooking 10 minutes   serves 4

---

*4 zucchini, yellow &
green, sliced ⅛-inch
(3mm) thick
Salt
1 cup all purpose flour
Vegetable oil for frying*

Lightly salt the zucchini slices. Place the flour in a large plastic bag. Add the zucchini to the bag and seal shut. Shake the bag so that the zucchini slices are coated in flour.

Pour enough vegetable oil into a large heavy saucepan to create a depth of 1-inch (2.5 cm). Heat the oil over high heat.

Working in batches, place the zucchini slices in the hot oil. Do not overcrowd. Fry until lightly golden-brown.

Use a slotted spoon to remove the zucchini chips from the oil and transfer to a plate lined with paper towel to absorb the excess oil.

Transfer to a serving platter and serve immediately while still hot and crispy.

Soups can be a starter dish, or they can be a meal. In our home, it was always the latter. With hearty multigrain bread, olives, cheese, and any one of the appetizers in this book, a soup can become the main dish of a fulfilling dinner.

Most of the soup recipes in this book do not use stock, preferring fresh tomato sauce and water as a base. They are hearty and satisfying without unnecessary saturated fats and sodium!

This chapter also offers a wide range of refreshing salads to compliment many meals. For the best results, aim to find the freshest ingredients possible.

Soups & Salads

Tomato Bean Soup

Lentil Soup

Tomato Fennel Soup

Chicken Soup

Chickpea Soup with Cumin

Smoked Cod Soup

Meatball Soup

Garlic Beet Salad

Potato & White Bean Salad

Tomato & Cucumber Village Salad

Bread Salad with Asparagus & Tomatoes

Traditional Greek Salad

Roasted Pepper Salad

Octopus Salad

Pasta Salad

Tomato Bean Soup

Fassolada (Fah-soh-LAH-dah)

This is the national dish of Greece, a simple, inexpensive bowl of bean soup. In Greece, this soup can be found in the most casual of taverns or in five-star restaurants. We enjoy this soup accompanied with feta cheese, anchovies and onion wedges.

preparation overnight soaking + 15 minutes   cooking 1 hour   serves 4

1 ½ cups navy beans, dried
1 tbsp baking soda
6 cups water
1 cup crushed tomato sauce
¼ cup olive oil
1 carrot, chopped
1 celery, chopped
1 yellow onion, minced
1 small potato, peeled
1 tsp fresh ginger, minced
1 tsp red pepper flakes
1 bay leaf
1 ½ tsp salt, plus to taste
Juice of ½ lemon
½ cup fresh parsley, chopped
½ cup feta cheese, crumbled
2 preserved anchovy fillets, minced (optional)
Lemon wedges (optional)

Place the beans in a large bowl, cover with water and let the beans soak overnight.

Drain the beans and transfer to a large stockpot. Cover with water and add the baking soda. Bring the beans to a boil over high heat for 5 minutes. Drain again and replace with 6 cups fresh water.

Add the crushed tomato sauce, olive oil, carrot, celery, onion, potato, ginger, red pepper flakes, bay leaf, and salt to the stockpot. Bring to a boil over high heat. Reduce heat and simmer for at least one hour, or until the beans are fork tender. Remove from the heat.

Discard the bay leaf and remove the potato. Place the potato in a food processor along with 1cup of soup. Purée until smooth. Return the purée to the pot and stir.

Taste and adjust the seasonings if necessary.

Add the lemon juice, parsley, and crumbled feta to the soup and stir. Serve warm.

Top each bowl with some chopped anchovies if desired and a lemon wedge.

SALT INTAKE
This recipe does not use stock or any canned items which tend to be high in sodium. If you are using canned substitutions then you will need to adjust the amount of salt being added.

TRY THIS! In our house we sometimes serve this soup with red onion or Vidalia wedges. The wedges are used to scoop up the soup like a spoon. You may not choose to eat the whole bowl in this manner but go ahead and give it a try!

Lentil Soup

Fakies (Fah-kee-EHS)

Lentils come in a variety of colours, the most commonly used lentils in Greece being brown. Unlike other dry beans, lentils do not need to be soaked overnight, making them a quick meal solution when you are tight on time. Lentils are fibre and iron rich, so make this quick and easy soup and serve often.

preparation 10 minutes   cooking 45 minutes   serves 4

1/3 cup olive oil
1 cup brown lentils, dried
1 yellow onion, minced
3 garlic cloves, minced
1 carrot, minced
1 celery, minced
2 bay leaves
1 tsp oregano, dried
1 tsp salt, plus to taste
Pepper, as desired
6 cups water
Olive oil for drizzling
Red wine vinegar, as desired
Kalamata olives (optional)

Heat the olive oil in a large pot over medium-high heat. Add the lentils, onion and garlic and sauté for 3 minutes.

Add the carrots and celery and sauté for 2 minutes further.

Add the bay leaves, oregano, salt and pepper and stir.

Add the water and bring to a boil. Reduce the heat and simmer for 45 minutes, or until the lentils are soft. If the soup becomes too thick, just add some hot water.

Discard the bay leaves before serving and adjust the seasonings if needed.

Ladle the soup into bowls and drizzle with olive oil. Add a teaspoon of red wine vinegar to each bowl if desired. Garnish with some olives and serve.

Tomato Fennel Soup

Soopa me Domata ke Maratho (SOO-pah meh Doh-MAH-tah keh MAH-rah-thoh)

If you have never cooked with fennel then here is your chance to try it. Fennel has a lovely anise flavour and is very refreshing when paired with ripe rich tomatoes.

preparation 15 minutes   cooking 30 minutes   serves 4   broil 500°F (260°C)

½ fennel bulb
2 tbsp olive oil
2 garlic cloves, minced
1 tsp fennel seeds
4 cups crushed tomato sauce
1 cup vegetable broth or water
¼ tsp salt
Pepper, as desired
1 baguette, sliced 1-inch (2.5cm) thick
10 Kalamata olives, pits removed
¼ cup feta cheese, crumbled
4 cherry tomatoes, halved
Basil leaves

Remove the tough inner core from the fennel bulb and coarsely chop. Heat the olive oil in a large saucepan over medium heat. Add the fennel to the saucepan. Cook for 4-5 minutes, until the fennel begins to soften. Add the garlic and fennel seeds and cook for 2 minutes further.

Add the tomato sauce and vegetable broth. Bring to a boil over high heat. Reduce heat and simmer for 30 minutes.

Purée the soup using a hand blender. Stir in the salt and pepper. Keep the soup warm while preparing the bread topping.

Place the bread on a baking sheet and broil in a preheated oven until the bread is browned on both sides, about 3 minutes per side. In a separate bowl mix the olives, feta and tomatoes together.

Ladle the soup into bowls, top with the toasted bread, and a scoop of the feta and olive mixture. Garnish with a basil leaf.

TIP
To use up all of your fennel, double the recipe and freeze a batch.

MAKE AHEAD
The soup can be made 3 days in advance and stored in the refrigerator. It can be stored in the freezer for up to 1 month.

Chicken Soup

Kotosoupa Avgolemmono (Koh-TOH-soo-pah Ahv-goh-LEH-moh-noh)

This is the dish that floods us with memories of our childhood. When any of us were ill and sent home early from school, this soup immediately began simmering on our stovetop. Definitely a kid favourite, though adults love it just as much! It is so creamy and comforting you will want to make it again and again.

---

preparation 15 minutes   cooking 2 hours   serves 4

---

4 chicken legs & 4 thighs,
about 1 lb (500g) total,
bone-in, skins removed
6 cups water
1 yellow onion, minced
1 carrot, chopped
1 celery, chopped
1 tsp oregano, dried
2 tbsp olive oil
1½ tsp salt
1 cup Arborio rice
Pepper, as desired

Lemon & Egg Sauce
recipe, see page 260

In a large pot, add the chicken and water and bring to a boil over high heat. Use a spoon to skim the impurities that rise to the surface. Reduce the heat and simmer for 60 minutes.

Remove the chicken from the pot and place in a bowl. When the chicken is cool enough to handle, remove the bones and discard. Set the cooled meat aside.

The liquid in the pot will have reduced. Fill the pot with hot water so that the level of water in the pot is roughly the same as when you started.

Add the onion, carrot, celery, oregano, oil and salt to the pot and cook over medium heat for 30 minutes. Remove 1 cup of broth from the pot and set aside.

Add the rice and simmer until the rice is soft and cooked through. This will take about 20 minutes. Add a little more water if the rice is uncooked and continue simmering.

Return the chicken to the pot. Taste and adjust the seasonings. Season with cracked pepper.

Prepare the *Lemon & Egg sauce* using the 1 cup of broth set aside earlier. Add the sauce to the pot and heat through over medium heat. Serve.

Chickpea Soup with Cumin

Revithosoupa (Reh-vee-THOH-soo-pah)

Jalapeños add a refreshing kick to this satisfying soup filled with wholesome veggies. This soup is so easy to make—and so good. Eating well can really be simple.

preparation 15 minutes   cooking 35 minutes   serves 6

2 tbsp olive oil
1 yellow onion, minced
1 carrot, chopped
1 celery, chopped
1 Jalapeño pepper, deseeded, chopped
½ tsp cumin seeds
1 tsp sweet paprika
4 cups chickpeas, cooked
4 cups water
1 cup crushed tomato sauce
1 tsp salt, plus to taste
½ cup fresh parsley, chopped

Heat the olive oil in a large pot over medium heat. Add the onion, carrot, celery and Jalapeño pepper and sauté for 3-4 minutes. Add the cumin seeds, paprika and sauté for 1 minute.

Add the chickpeas, water, crushed tomato sauce and salt to the pot. Increase the heat and bring the ingredients to a boil. Reduce the heat and simmer for 30-35 minutes. Remove from the heat. Taste and adjust the seasonings if needed.

Ladle half of the soup into a food processor and purée. Return the purée to the pot and mix.

Add the chopped parsley and give it a quick stir.

Serve warm.

Smoked Cod Soup

Psarosoupa (Psah-ROH-soo-pah)

Our mom's favourite winter time soup—probably because it takes little effort to make but is pleasing even to those who usually avoid fish. The smoky flavour of the cod infuses the vegetable broth, which is then freshened up with lemon for a flavour that is really unique.

preparation 15 minutes   cooking 30 minutes   serves 4

2 cups potatoes, peeled, cut into 1½-inch (4cm) cubes
2 carrots, chopped
2 celery, chopped
1 yellow onion, minced
1/3 cup olive oil
4 cups water
1 cup smoked cod, cut into 2-inch (5cm) pieces
1 tbsp fresh parsley, chopped
1 tsp salt, plus to taste
Pepper, as desired
Juice of ½ lemon

VARIATION
If you like the smoky flavour then try smoked salmon for a change. If you don't like the smoky flavour, try fresh cod or salmon fillets instead.

In a large pot add the potatoes, carrots, celery, onion, and olive oil. Cover with 4 cups water and bring to a boil over high heat. Reduce the heat and simmer for 15 minutes.

Add the fish, parsley and salt. Bring to a boil, then reduce the heat and simmer for 10 minutes.

The vegetables should be fork tender and the fish should be flaky. Adjust the salt if needed, add pepper to taste and squeeze in the lemon juice. Give it a quick stir and serve.

Meatball Soup

Yiouverlakia (Yee-ou-vehr-LAH-kee-ah)

This is comfort food—rice and beef meatballs topped with creamy *Lemon & Egg Sauce*. Enjoy with fresh bread.

---

preparation 30 minutes   cooking 30 minutes   serves 6

---

1 lb (500g) ground beef, extra lean
1 yellow onion, minced
½ cup Arborio rice
½ cup fresh parsley, chopped
1 egg
1 tsp salt
Pepper as desired
4 cups water
¼ cup olive oil
½ tsp salt

Lemon & Egg Sauce recipe, see page 260.

Add the beef, onion, rice, parsley, egg, salt and pepper to a medium-sized bowl. Mix the ingredients together thoroughly with your hands. Shape the beef mixture into bite-sized balls and set aside.

Fill a large pot half-way with water and bring to a rapid boil. Add the meatballs to the boiling water and reduce the heat. Low-boil for 10 minutes. Remove the meatballs from the water and set aside. Discard the water and fatty liquid that was released from the meatballs.

Clean the pot and add 4 cups of fresh water to the pot. Bring the water to a rapid boil over high heat. Add the meatballs, olive oil and salt. Reduce the heat and simmer for 20 minutes until the rice is cooked through.

Prepare the *Lemon & Egg Sauce* and add it to the pot. Heat through.

Serve immediately.

Garlic Beet Salad

Padzaria (Pah-DZAH-ree-ah)

Beautiful, vibrant, red beets; we love them all year round, especially when paired with grilled fish.

preparation 15 minutes	cooking 1 hour 10 minutes	serves 4	bake 400°F (200°C)

4 beets with greens,
about 5oz (155g) each
¼ cup olive oil
3 tbsp red wine vinegar
2 garlic cloves, pressed
½ tsp oregano, dried
½ tsp salt

TIP
Wear rubber gloves to
avoid staining fingertips
when peeling beets.

Remove the leafy beet greens and red stalks and set aside. Cut the roots off of the beets and discard. Scrub the beets well under cold water and wrap individually in foil. Place on a baking sheet and roast in a preheated oven for 60 minutes or until fork tender.

When cool enough to handle, remove the foil and rub the beets with your hands to remove the skins; the skins should slip off easily. Slice the beets and place on a serving platter. Set aside.

Wash the beet greens and stalks that were set aside earlier and cut them into thirds. Discard any leafy part that is wilted or brown.

Place the stalks and greens in a large pot. Cover the greens with water and bring to a boil over high heat. Reduce the heat and simmer for 10 minutes or until tender.

Strain the greens and transfer to the same platter with the beets.

Whisk the oil, vinegar, crushed garlic, oregano and salt together in a small bowl. Pour the vinaigrette on the warm sliced beets and greens. The beets will draw in the vinaigrette best when they are warm. Marinate for a few hours.

The salad may be served warm or cold on their own, with crumbled feta or cottage cheese.

Potato & White Bean Salad

Salata me Patates ke Fassolia (Sah-LAH-tah meh Pah-TAH-tes keh Fah-SOH-lee-ah)

In our home, many Greek vegetarian dishes were borne out of Lent—Sarakosti—when no meat is eaten for forty days. This dish was a Lent favourite because it was always very hearty and filling.
In the summer, we enjoy it often with barbequed meat and fish.

---

preparation 20 minutes   cooking 20 minutes   serves 4   bake 425°F (220°C)

1lb (500g) fingerling potatoes
2 tbsp olive oil
½ tsp salt
2 cups white beans, cooked
2 tbsp capers
10 Kalamata olives, pits removed
6 scallions, chopped both white & green
½ cup each fresh parsley & basil, chopped
2 tbsp fresh dill, chopped
¼ cup feta cheese, crumbled

FOR THE DRESSING
1/3 cup olive oil
Juice of 1 lemon
1 tbsp Dijon mustard
¼ cup yogurt, Greek or Balkan Style
1 preserved anchovy fillet, rinsed & chopped
Pepper, as desired

Place the potatoes in a roasting pan. Drizzle with olive oil and season with salt. Roast for 20 minutes in a preheated oven, or until the potatoes are fork tender.

When the potatoes are cool enough to handle, cut them into bite-sized pieces and place in a salad bowl.

Add the beans, capers, olives, scallions, fresh herbs and feta cheese to the salad bowl.

Whisk the dressing ingredients together in a small mixing bowl.

Toss the salad with the dressing.

Let the salad sit for at least one hour before serving.

Tomato & Cucumber Village Salad

Horiatiki Salata (Hoh-ree-AH-tee-kee Sah-LAH-tah)

This refreshing salad is enjoyed almost daily in Greek homes throughout the summer, when tomatoes are at their peak. Use only the freshest ingredients and the juiciest tomatoes you can find. The best accompaniment to this dish is warm, crunchy bread. The juice of the ripe tomatoes mixed with olive oil and crumbled feta is to die for!

---

preparation 10 minutes   serves 4

---

3 tomatoes, cut into wedges
1 cucumber, peeled & chopped
½ Vidalia onion, sliced
¼ cup olive oil
½ cup feta cheese, crumbled
½ tsp oregano, dried
¼ tsp salt

Toss all of the ingredients together in a salad bowl

Serve with bread.

VARIATION
Add 2 boiled potatoes to this salad. Quarter them and season with salt.

Bread Salad with Asparagus & Tomatoes

Salata me Psomi ke Sparagia (Sah-LAH-tah meh Psoh-MEE keh Spah-RAH-guee-AH)

A great salad to make when you have leftover bread. Day-old bread works best because it absorbs the vinaigrette without getting too soggy. Really easy to make and really good. This salad is a winner.

preparation 10 minutes   cooking 8 minutes   serves 4   broil 500°F (260°C)

1 cup asparagus, chopped, 1-inch (2.5cm) pieces
1 tbsp olive oil
Pinch of salt
4 cups day old bread, cut into 1-inch (2.5cm) cubes
2 tomatoes, cut into wedges
½ cucumber, peeled and chopped
½ cup feta cheese, crumbled
8 basil leaves, chopped

FOR THE DRESSING
1/3 cup olive oil
2 tbsp balsamic vinegar
1 tbsp red wine vinegar
¼ tsp oregano, dried
¼ tsp salt

Place the asparagus on a baking sheet, drizzle with the olive oil and sprinkle with salt. Place in a preheated oven and broil for 4 minutes on one side, turn and broil for 4 minutes further. Remove from the oven and set aside to cool.

Add the remaining salad ingredients to a salad bowl, along with the cooled asparagus.

In a small bowl, whisk the dressing ingredients and pour over the salad. Toss and let the salad sit for 15 minutes to allow the bread to absorb the dressing. Serve.

Traditional Greek Salad

Maroulosalata (Mah-roo-loh-sah-LAH-tah)

Our dad is a pretty traditional guy, so this is his favourite salad. The secret to this salad is to finely chop the lettuce leaves and use your hands to massage the dressing into the lettuce. This is the perfect salad to serve with *Santorini-Style Souvlaki on a Pita*. Very refreshing.

preparation 8 minutes   serves 6

1 bunch romaine lettuce,
1lb (500g), chopped
¼-inch (6mm) thick
1 cucumber, sliced
1 tomato, cut into
wedges

FOR THE DRESSING
1/3 cup olive oil
3 tbsp red wine vinegar
1 tsp oregano, dried
½ tsp salt

½ cup feta cheese,
crumbled

¼ cup Marinated Olives
recipe, see page 51

Place the finely chopped lettuce in a salad bowl. Add the cucumber and tomatoes.

Combine the dressing ingredients in a small mixing bowl.

Pour the dressing over the salad and use your hands to massage the dressing into the lettuce.

Top the salad with the feta cheese and marinated olives. Serve.

VARIATION
Substitute romaine lettuce with iceberg lettuce.

Roasted Pepper Salad

Salata me Psimenes Piperies (Sah-LAH-tah meh Psee-MEH-nehs Pee-peh-ree-EHS)

The smell of red peppers roasting will bring the Mediterranean into your home. Although you can easily find red peppers in jars at the grocery store, you will not regret taking the time to roast them yourself. This is a refreshing, colourful and elegant salad.

---

preparation 20 minutes   cooking 15 minutes   serves 4

---

3 red peppers, whole

FOR THE DRESSING
1 shallot, minced
1 tbsp balsamic vinegar
1 tbsp cider vinegar
¼ cup olive oil
¼ tsp each salt & pepper

4 cups baby spinach
¼ cup goat cheese, crumbled

MAKE AHEAD
The red peppers can be marinating in the dressing the night before serving day until ready to combine with the spinach.

Place the peppers whole on a preheated grill.

Remove from grill when charred black on all sides. Place the peppers in a bowl and set aside for 10 minutes. When the skins of the peppers have wrinkled, peel and seed them. Cut them into slices. Add the peppers along with the pepper juices to a salad bowl.

Prepare the dressing and drizzle it on top of the peppers. Mix and set aside for 10 minutes.

Place the spinach in a salad bowl, add the peppers and toss to coat the spinach with the dressing. Top the salad with the crumbled goat cheese and serve.

FREEZING TIP
Roasted peppers freeze very well. Roast and peel the peppers. Let them cool, and then place them in a container with their juices and a touch of olive oil. Freeze them in small batches to enjoy later in salads, pasta, on pizza, or in sandwiches.

Octopus Salad

Salata me Ohtapodi (Sah-LAH-tah meh Oh-htah-POH-dee)

Eating seaside is the best way to enjoy octopus, but a backyard filled with friendly faces is the next best thing. This dish is surprisingly easy to make and very impressive!

---

preparation 25 minutes + 2 hours marinating time   cooking 60 minutes   serves 6

---

1 octopus, 3lb (1.5kg)
2 carrots, minced
2 celery, minced
½ red onion, minced
12 cherry tomatoes

FOR THE DRESSING
¼ cup olive oil
¼ cup fresh lemon juice
2 tbsp red wine vinegar
1 garlic clove, pressed
¼ tsp salt
1 tbsp fresh parsley, chopped
½ tsp oregano, dried
¼ cup feta cheese, crumbled (optional)

Remove the head and beak from the octopus using a sharp knife and discard. Rinse the octopus.

Place the octopus in a large pot and cover with water. Low-boil the octopus for 60 minutes, or until it is tender. Drain. Transfer to a cutting board and let it cool. Discard the sac and cut the tentacles into bite-sized pieces and place in a salad bowl.

Add the carrots, celery, onion and tomatoes to the salad bowl.

Combine the dressing ingredients in a small mixing bowl and pour over the salad. Let the salad marinate at room temperature for 2 hours before serving.

Just before serving, top the salad with parsley, oregano and crumbled feta cheese if desired.

Pasta Salad

Salata me Pasta (Sah-LAH-tah meh PAH-stah)

The longer this salad marinates, the better it tastes. It's perfect for a potluck or picnic lunch.

---

preparation 20 minutes   serves 4

---

4 cups rotini pasta, dried
1 jar marinated
artichokes, 6 floz (170ml)
1 jar marinated
mushrooms, 8.5 floz
(250ml), drained
½ cup feta cheese,
crumbled
12 Kalamata olives, pits
removed, chopped
12 cherry tomatoes

FOR THE DRESSING
¼ cup marinated
artichoke liquid
¼ cup olive oil
¼ cup red wine vinegar
1 garlic clove, sliced
¼ tsp each salt & pepper

¼ cup each fresh basil &
oregano, chopped

Cook the pasta in a pot of salted boiling water. Drain.

Add the cooked and cooled pasta to a large salad bowl.

Drain the artichokes and reserve the liquid for the dressing. Add the artichokes, mushrooms, feta cheese, olives and cherry tomatoes to the salad bowl.

Combine the dressing ingredients in a small mixing bowl and add to the salad bowl. Toss to coat. Let the salad marinate for 1 hour. Add the fresh herbs and serve.

Though known for their grilled meat dishes, Greeks can very easily be vegetarians, or at least our parents could be. In their childhood, our parents only ate meat a few times a year: pork at Christmas, lamb on Easter Sunday, and the odd rabbit or wild boar that was hunted in the months in between.

Vegetarian entrées were served often in our home growing up. In this chapter we have included our favourite vegetarian recipes. Some work well as an accompaniment to meat and fish, and others are vegetarian dishes that are meant to be served as a main meal.

Vegetarian Entrées or Side Dishes

Grilled Summer Vegetables

Stove-top Green Beans with Zucchini & Potatoes

Baked Elephant Beans

Sweet Spinach with Dill & Rice

Roasted Vegetables

1000 Layers of Vegetables

Black-eyed Peas with Kale & Lemon

Summer Greens

Artichokes & Potatoes with Dill

Zucchini Tart

Lemon Asparagus

Grilled Tomato Halves

Stuffed Tomatoes, Peppers & Zucchini Flowers

Grilled Summer Vegetables

Lahanika sti Shara (Lah-hah-nee-KAH stee SHAH-rah)

There is nothing quite like colourful grilled vegetables to announce the arrival of summer. Place them on a large platter for a cheerful side dish to be enjoyed with grilled meats. On their own, lay the grilled vegetables on top of a Greek pita, add a dollop of *Tsatziki*, and savour the flavours.

---

preparation 25 minutes   cooking 10 minutes   serves 6

---

3 Japanese eggplants, sliced ¼-inch (6mm) thick
Salt
2 zucchini, sliced ¼-inch (6mm) thick
Olive oil for brushing
1 red onion, sliced ¼-inch (6mm) thick
12 white button mushrooms, whole
2 red or yellow peppers, whole

FOR THE VINAIGRETTE
½ cup olive oil
¼ cup red wine vinegar
1 garlic clove, pressed
1 tsp oregano, dried
½ tsp salt
8 basil leaves, chopped

MAKE AHEAD
Grilled Summer Vegetables can be made one day in advance and stored in the refrigerator. They can be served cold.

Place the eggplant slices on a flat work surface and lightly salt them. Set aside for 20 minutes so that the salt can draw out the bitter juices. Pat the eggplant dry using a paper towel.

Brush the eggplant and zucchini slices lightly with oil on both sides. Place the eggplant, zucchini, onion, mushrooms and peppers on a preheated grill. Mushrooms should be placed cap-side down on the grill.

Remove the eggplant, zucchini and onion from the grill once the vegetables are tender and lightly charred on both sides, about 8 minutes. Set aside in a glass bowl.

Remove the mushrooms when cooked on the cap-side, place in the same bowl as the other vegetables.

Peppers should be removed from the grill when charred black on all sides. Place the peppers in a separate bowl from the other vegetables and set aside for 10 minutes. When the skins of the peppers have wrinkled, peel and seed them and cut the peppers into slices ½-inch (12mm) thick. Add the peppers along with any pepper juices to the glass bowl.

Combine the vinaigrette ingredients together in a small mixing bowl. Drizzle over the warm vegetables and store any extra vinaigrette in the refrigerator for a later use.

Add the basil and serve warm or cold.

Stove-top Green Beans with Zucchini & Potatoes

Fassolakia Fresca (Fah-soh-LAH-kee-ah FREHS-kah)

This is one of our favourite dishes in the summertime when most of the ingredients can be freshly picked from the garden. Green beans, a perpetual side-dish, take centre-stage here and hold their own deliciously.

---

preparation 15 minutes   cooking 25 minutes   serves 4

1lb (500g) fresh green beans, trimmed at both ends
3 potatoes, quartered
1 cup crushed tomato sauce
1 yellow onion, diced
¼ cup olive oil
1 tsp salt
2 cups water
2 zucchini, cut into 1-inch (2.5cm) pieces
Feta cheese, crumbled or Mizithra or Pecorino Romano cheese, grated

Place the ingredients except for the zucchini and cheese in a large pot

Bring to a boil. Reduce the heat and simmer, covered, for 20 minutes.

Add the zucchini to the pot. Continue simmering for 5 minutes further or until the beans and zucchini are tender. Taste and adjust the seasonings if needed.

Top with cheese and serve warm with some bread.

Baked Elephant Beans

Yiyathes (YEE-yah-thes)

Elephant beans are the giants of the bean family, and in this classic Greek recipe they are baked with carrots, celery and tomatoes. This dish is healthy and delicious.

Elephant beans are indigenous to Greece. They are larger and meatier than lima beans, and have a more pronounced kidney shape. If you cannot find elephant beans, lima beans are an acceptable substitute. If you are a vegetarian, we highly recommend seeking these beans out. They are to beans what Portobello mushrooms are to mushrooms—big, hearty and filling.

---

preparation overnight soaking + 15 minutes   cooking 1 hour 30 minutes   serves 6   bake 400°F (200°C)

---

2 cups elephant beans or lima beans, dried
6 cups water
1 cup crushed tomato sauce
1 yellow onion, diced
2 carrots, chopped
2 celery sticks, chopped
1/3 cup olive oil
2 tbsp honey
2 bay leaves
1 tsp salt, plus to taste
Pepper, as desired
4 cups hot water

Place the beans in a large bowl with 6 cups of cold water and let them soak overnight.

Replace the water and boil the beans in a pot for 15 minutes. Drain. (This step will significantly reduce the cooking time in the oven.)

Place the beans in an oven-proof dish with a fitted lid. Ensure that the beans are not overcrowded otherwise they will become too mushy.

Add the remaining ingredients to the dish and give it a quick stir.

Place in a preheated oven and cook, covered, for 1 hour 30 minutes or until the beans are tender when pierced with a fork and the sauce is thick and creamy. Remove the bay leaves and serve.

Sweet Spinach with Dill & Rice

Spanakorizo (Spah-nah-KOH-ree-zoh)

This meal is as delicious as it is easy. Velvety sautéed spinach combined with Arborio rice make for a fulfilling light entrée. When topped with feta cheese it takes on a whole new dimension. The sweetness of the spinach plays off the saltiness of the feta—simply yummy!

---

preparation 15 minutes   cooking 20 minutes   serves 4

---

1 bunch fresh spinach,
1lb (500g), washed, white
stalks removed
2 tbsp olive oil
1 yellow onion, diced
Pinch of salt
1 tbsp fresh dill, chopped
1 cup Arborio rice
2 cups water
1 tsp salt
Juice of 1 lemon
Olive oil for drizzling
Feta cheese, crumbled
(optional)
4 lemon wedges

Cut the spinach in half and set aside.

Heat the olive oil in a heavy saucepan over medium heat. Add the onions and a pinch of salt. Sauté onions until soft, about 5 minutes.

Add all of the spinach to the pan a handful at a time and sauté. Add the dill, rice, 2 cups of water and salt. Bring to a boil.

Reduce the heat and simmer, covered, until the water is absorbed, about 20 minutes. If the rice is not tender and fluffy at this point, add more hot water and continue simmering.

Remove the pan from the heat. Add the lemon juice and drizzle with some olive oil.

Serve warm or at room temperature. Top with some crumbled feta cheese if desired and garnish with a lemon wedge just before serving.

Roasted Vegetables

Psita Lahanika sto Fourno (Psee-TAH Lah-hah-nee-KAH stoh FOOR-noh)

The hardest part of this dish is waiting 45 minutes for it to be cooked. You simply throw all the wonderful ingredients together, place them in the oven and let them roast. We suggest you add 6 cloves of garlic but you needn't stop there, add a whole head of garlic if you dare.

---

preparation 15 minutes   cooking 45 minutes   serves 6   bake 400°F (200°C)

---

1 cup okra, fresh or frozen
1 eggplant, cut into 2-inch (5cm) pieces
2 red peppers, quartered
2 Vidalia or red onions, quartered
3 sweet potatoes, peeled, cut into 2-inch (5cm) pieces
6 garlic cloves, whole
1/3 cup olive oil
¼ cup balsamic vinegar
2 tsp thyme, dried
1 tsp oregano, dried
1 tsp salt
Pepper, as desired

Place all of the vegetables in a roasting pan large enough to arrange the vegetables in a single layer.

In a small bowl, whisk the olive oil, balsamic vinegar, thyme, oregano and salt. Drizzle over the vegetables.

Roast for 45 minutes in a preheated oven or until all of the vegetables are fork tender. Be sure not to stir the vegetables while they roast, as this will break apart the vegetables.

Season with pepper and serve warm .

1000 Layers of Vegetables

Hilies Strosis apo Lahanika (HEE-lee-ehs STROH-sees ah-POH Lah-hah-nee-KAH)

We may have exaggerated the number of layers, but this dish is truly beautiful. Layers of zucchini and tomatoes are stacked together and then topped with goat cheese. The impressive look of this dish matches its taste.

preparation 20 minutes	cooking 20 minutes	serves 4	bake 350°F (180°C)

2 tbsp olive oil
2 zucchini, sliced ⅛-inch (3mm) thick
Pinch of salt
1 tbsp fresh thyme, minced
2 garlic cloves, sliced
3 tomatoes, sliced ¼-inch (6mm) thick
Pinch of salt
1 tbsp fresh basil, minced
1 tsp oregano, dried
4 slices goat cheese, cut ¼-inch (6mm) thick
Pepper, as desired

MAKE AHEAD
The layered vegetables can be assembled and refrigerated on the morning of serving day. Bake just before serving.

Heat 1 tablespoon of the olive oil in a small sauté pan over medium heat. Add the zucchini slices, salt and thyme. Sauté until the zucchini has softened, about 8 minutes. Remove from the heat and set the ingredients aside in a small bowl.

In the same sauté pan, heat the remaining olive oil and add the garlic slices. Sauté for 1 minute. Add the tomato slices, salt, basil and oregano. Sauté until the tomatoes are softened, about 3 minutes. Remove from the heat and set aside in a separate bowl.

Alternate layering the zucchini and tomatoes using an open-bottomed cylindrical ramekin. Finish with a layer of goat cheese.

Place the layered vegetables on a parchment paper-lined baking sheet in the middle of a preheated oven. Bake for 20 minutes, until the ingredients have warmed through and the goat cheese has melted.

Use a spatula to transfer the layered vegetables to a serving plate. Serve.

Black-Eyed Peas with Kale & Lemon

Mavromatika Fassolia me Katsaro Lahano

(Mah-vroh-MAH-tee-kah Fah-SOH-lee-ah meh Kah-tsah-ROH LAH-hah-noh)

We love this dish and our kids adore it. Its high protein, iron and fibre content, combined with low fat and low calories, will please the most diet conscious cooks. Boosted up with a chili pepper kick, kale never tasted better!

---

preparation 10 minutes   cooking 25 minutes   serves 4

---

3 tbsp olive oil
1 yellow onion, diced
Pinch of salt
1 bunch kale, 1lb (500g), washed, tough stalks removed, cut into 1-inch (2.5cm) pieces
2 chili peppers, dried
2 cups water
1 cup black-eyed peas, cooked
¼ tsp salt
Olive oil for drizzling
Juice of 1 lemon
Pepper, as desired

COOKING PEAS
Soak peas in water for 4-6 hours or overnight. Discard water and place in a pot of boiling water. Boil for 30 minutes or until beans are tender. Strain and add to any dish. Unused cooked peas can be stored in the refrigerator for 3 days or in the freezer for up to 3 months.

Heat the olive oil in a large pot with a fitted lid over medium heat. Add the onion and a pinch of salt and sauté until soft, about 5 minutes.

Add all of the kale to the pot a handful at a time. It will begin to wilt and the volume will reduce significantly. Drop the chili peppers into the pot and pour at least 2 cups of water, so that the kale is almost submerged. Cook over medium-low heat, partially covered, for 20 minutes or until the kale is cooked through. The kale should retain its lovely green colour and still be a bit crunchy. Add the peas, salt and continue cooking for 5 minutes until warmed through. Remove pot from heat.

You may use a slotted spoon to remove the kale and peas and serve as a side dish or you can serve it as a hearty meal and eat it with a piece of crunchy bread. If desired, drizzle olive oil in the pot or into each individual bowl.

Add the lemon juice and pepper to taste immediately before serving. Serve warm.

Summer Greens

Horta (HOR-tah)

Dandelion greens—that pesky backyard nuisance—are actually a powerhouse of nutrients. Picked before they flower, dandelion greens are tender once cooked. Serve them with grilled or fried fish for a truly Greek summer meal.

---

preparation 10 minutes   cooking 20 minutes   serves 4-6

---

1 bunch dandelion greens, 1lb (500g)
¼ cup olive oil
1 garlic clove, sliced
4-6 lemon wedges

SUBSTITUTIONS
Dandelions can be substituted with amaranth (*vlita*), chicory (*radiki*), sorrel (*lapata*), and even spinach (*spanaki*).
All are green, all are packed with nutrients, and all are delicious!

Rinse the dandelions in a cold water bath. Dandelion greens need thorough washing, exchange the water at least three times.

Cut off the white ends of the dandelions and discard. Discard any brown or wilted greens. Cut the greens into thirds and place in a large pot of salted boiling water for 10-15 minutes.

Remove the dandelion greens from the water and place in a large bowl.

In a small bowl, mix the olive oil and garlic. Drizzle over the hot greens.

Squeeze lemon juice on each individual plate just before serving.

Serve warm or cold on the side of any dish or enjoy as a light lunch.

Artichokes & Potatoes with Dill

Aginares me Patates (Ah-guee-NAH-res meh Pah-TAH-tehs)

If you are reluctant about preparing fresh artichokes, since they are somewhat uncommon in North American cuisine, then please go ahead and use water packed artichokes. Whatever you do—DO TRY THIS DISH! It is one of the most elegant vegetarian dishes out there. Delectable.

preparation 30 minutes   cooking 30 minutes   serves 6

¼ cup olive oil
1 yellow onion, minced
6 small potatoes, 1½ lb (750g), peeled, cut into 1-inch (2.5 cm) cubes
2 cups water
1 tsp salt, plus to taste
1 tbsp fresh dill, chopped
10 artichokes, cleaned, halved (tips on preparing artichokes, next page)
1½ cups water

Lemon & Egg Sauce
recipe, see page 260

Pepper, as desired

SUBSTITUTIONS
Substitute fresh artichokes with frozen or canned ones. If using canned artichokes be sure they are packed in water. These artichokes are pre-cooked and should be simmered in the pot for the last 5 minutes of cooking time. The water should also be reduced by ½ cup.

Heat the olive oil in a wide-bottomed pot over medium heat. Add the onions and sauté until soft, about 5 minutes.

Add the potatoes and sauté for 1 minute.

Add water to almost cover the potatoes, about 2 cups. Add the salt and dill and bring to a boil. Reduce the heat and simmer for 10 minutes.

Add the artichokes and 1½ cups water. Bring to a boil and then reduce the heat and simmer for 10 minutes or until all of the vegetables are perfectly cooked through and fork tender. Remove from the heat.

Prepare the Lemon and Egg Sauce.

Add the Lemon and Egg Sauce to the pot over medium heat. Remove from the heat just before it reaches a boil. Grind pepper to taste and adjust the salt if necessary.

Serve warm.

MAKE AHEAD
Cleaned artichokes can sit in the lemon water bath all day until ready to be cooked.

PREPARING THE ARTICHOKES

Prepare a large bowl of cold water with some lemon slices and freshly squeezed lemon juice. Set aside. Trim the stem off the artichoke. Snap back the hard green leaves with your fingers until you reach the tender lighter greenish-yellow inner layer of leaves. Cut the artichoke in half and scoop out the fuzzy "choke" part. Trim away the tip of the artichoke and remove any other dark green coloured parts. Submerge into the cold lemon water bath.

Zucchini Tart

Tourta me Kolokithia (TOOR-tah meh Koh-loh-KEE-thee-ah)

Our parents' garden was a reflection of what they held dear to their hearts—their native homeland. They weren't able to bring back the mountains and the breathtaking views of the ocean that Greece offered them, but they were able to grow most of the vegetables and herbs that they enjoyed eating there. Growing up, we had pots of eggplant growing beside basil, we had grape vines giving us shade and tasty fruit, and we had bean stalks and zucchini plants as high as our fence.
The three of us enjoy tending our own gardens almost as much as our parents. If there is an abundance of ripe zucchini on a given day we often throw them all together and make a delicious tart.

---

preparation 15 minutes   cooking 40 minutes   serves 4   bake 350°F (180°C)

---

1 deep dish tart shell, 9-inch (23cm)
2 tbsp olive oil
3 zucchini, 1lb (500g), sliced ⅛-inch (3mm) thick
4 scallions, chopped, both white and green
2 garlic cloves, minced
2 tbsp fresh mint, chopped
¼ tsp each salt & pepper
½ cup feta cheese, crumbled
2 eggs
1/3 cup cream, 10%

Use a fork to poke holes along the bottom of the tart shell. Place in a preheated oven and bake for 10 minutes. Set aside to cool.

Heat the olive oil in a large frying pan over medium heat. Add the zucchini and scallions and sauté for 3 minutes. Add the garlic and sauté until the juices in the frying pan have evaporated. Add the mint, salt and pepper. Remove the pan from the heat and stir in the feta cheese.

Scoop half of the mixture into the prepared tart shell.

In a small bowl, whisk the eggs and cream together. Pour half of the mixture into the tart shell.

Add the remaining zucchini mixture to the tart shell and top with the remaining eggs and cream.

Place the tart in a preheated oven and bake for 35 minutes until the pie has set and the eggs and cream are stiff.

Remove from the oven and let cool for 5 minutes before cutting and serving.

Lemon Asparagus

Sparagia me Lemoni (Spah-RAH-guee-ah meh Leh-MOH-nee)

Simple and elegant—the perfect side dish.

---

preparation 5 minutes   cooking 8 minutes   serves 4   broil 500°F (260°C)

---

1 bunch asparagus, 1 lb (500g), tough ends removed
2 tbsp olive oil
¼ tsp each salt & pepper
Juice of ½ lemon

Place the trimmed asparagus on a baking sheet. Drizzle with the olive oil and season with salt and pepper.

Place in the upper third of a preheated oven and cook for 3-4 minutes on each side, until tender.

Transfer to a serving platter and squeeze the lemon juice over the hot asparagus.

Serve warm.

Grilled Tomato Halves

Domates sti Shara (Doh-MAH-tehs stee SHAH-rah)

Summer just wouldn't be the same without sweet, aromatic tomatoes. In our home, our tomato plants would grow as high as our chests alongside giant terracotta pots of basil. On warm summer evenings when we brought the two together, it was magic.

preparation 15 minutes   cooking 5 minutes   serves 4

Olive oil
4 tomatoes, halved
Coarse sea salt
1 tbsp fresh basil, chopped
1 garlic clove, minced

Use a brush to lightly coat a grill with olive oil.

Place the tomatoes on the preheated grill over medium-high heat. Grill on both sides for 8 minutes total, or until the tomatoes are warmed through but still retain their shape.

Transfer the tomatoes to a serving platter. Sprinkle the tops of the tomatoes with salt, basil and garlic.

Serve immediately.

Stuffed Tomatoes, Peppers & Zucchini Flowers

Yemista (Yeh-mee-STAH)

Our parents grew tomatoes and zucchini plants in their backyard every summer. As children we would help pick and stuff them with rice, fresh mint, parsley, and onions. This colourful dish is cheerful and summery. For the three of us, the aroma of it cooking floods our minds and hearts with fond memories. On one of many summer vacations spent in Greece visiting family, we learned the secret to this dish – sautéed onions and lots of them. Our aunts picked vegetables first thing in the morning, stuffed them, and then dropped off a large roasting pan at the nearby bakery. After a day of swimming, sunbathing and sipping on frappé we drove by the bakery to retrieve our dinner. Back at the summer home under a canopy of grape vines, we dined while looking into the faces of family from whom we felt so much love.

preparation 30 minutes	cooking 1 hour 15 minutes	serves 6	bake 425°F (220°C)

8 tomatoes, whole
4 yellow & red bell
Peppers, whole
Zucchini flowers
(optional)
¼ cup olive oil
2 yellow onions, minced
Pinch of salt
1½ tsp salt
¼ tsp pepper
1 cup Arborio rice
1/3 cup fresh mint,
chopped
¼ cup fresh parsley,
chopped

Using a sharp tomato knife, slice off the tops of the tomatoes to make a lid. If possible, try not to cut the lid off completely. Remove the tough inner core of the tomato.

Scoop the soft flesh of the tomatoes with a spoon and place in a large bowl. Purée the flesh with a hand blender or simply use your hands.

Make lids for the peppers and seed them.

If using, wash the zucchini flowers.

Arrange the hollowed vegetables in a roasting pan with a fitted lid so that the vegetables fit snugly and are holding each other up.

Heat 2 tablespoons of the olive oil in a sauté pan and add the onions and a pinch of salt. Sauté for 20 minutes over medium-low heat until the onions are soft and caramelized.

Add the onions to the bowl of tomato flesh. Season with salt and pepper. Stir in the rice, mint and parsley. This is the stuffing.

Completely fill the hollowed vegetables with the stuffing and place the lids back on the tomatoes and peppers.

Drizzle the remaining olive oil on top of the vegetables and into the roasting pan. Place the roasting pan, covered, in the middle of a preheated oven and cook for 60-75 minutes.

Remove the pan from the oven, remove the lid, and let the vegetables rest for 15-30 minutes before serving. Serve with some bread and a dollop of plain Greek or Balkan style yogurt.

HOW TO PICK ZUCCHINI FLOWERS
If you are growing zucchini in your backyard you will find bright yellow flowers open wide first thing in the morning. This is the time to pick them. As you remove the flowers from the plant, remove the stamen from the center of the flower.
Flowers should be stuffed the day they are picked.

Greeks make great potatoes. It is a vegetable that is almost always on the dinner table.

This chapter includes a variety of potato recipes that will quickly become family favourites.

There are essentially two ingredients you need to make great tasting potatoes: olive oil and salt. The olive oil must be of an excellent quality and the potato must be well seasoned. The rest comes with practice.

Potatoes

Garlic & Olive Oil Mashed Potatoes

Fried Potatoes

Red Roasted Potatoes

Cinnamon & Clove Potatoes

Paprika Potatoes

Lemon Potatoes

Garlic & Olive Oil Mashed Potatoes

Skordalia (Skor-dah-lee-AH)

What we love about these mashed potatoes is that they are made with an unconventional ingredient—white vinegar. We also use olive oil instead of butter and milk—so Greek, so garlicky, so good.

---

preparation 10 minutes   cooking 30 minutes   serves 6 as a side or makes 3 cups as a dip

---

8 yellow potatoes, 2 lbs
(1kg)
½ cup olive oil
2 tbsp white wine vinegar
4 garlic cloves, pressed
½ tsp salt

Peel the potatoes and cut them in half. Place in a large pot of boiling water until they are cooked through, about 30 minutes.

Drain the potatoes and add to a mixing bowl. Lightly mash the potatoes with a potato masher.

Whisk the olive oil, vinegar, garlic and salt in a small bowl and add to the potatoes. Vigorously mash the potatoes until they are creamy and smooth.

Taste and adjust the salt if needed.

The perfect pairing to this dish is a *Baked Cod with a Tomato Onion Relish* found on page 188, or you can enjoy it as an appetizer with breadsticks and pita wedges.

Fried Potatoes

Tiyanites Patates (Tee-yah-nee-TEHS Pah-TAH-tehs)

Our mom never used any fancy cooking gadgets, yet her meals were always cooked to perfection. The same was true with her fried potatoes. She abides by the following rules—if you drop a potato wedge into the hot oil and it sizzles, the oil is ready—if you drop a potato wedge into the oil and it begins to smoke, the oil is too hot, turn the heat down! Your frying pan should be deep, your potatoes should not be crowded and they should be cooked in batches. That is pretty much all you need to know.

preparation 10 minutes   cooking 30 minutes   serves 4

6 yellow potatoes, 1lb (500g)
Vegetable oil for frying
½ tsp salt

MAKE AHEAD
The potatoes can be fried for 4 minutes just so that the inside of the potato is cooked up to 2 hours before serving time. Just before serving, fry the potatoes in hot oil again until they are crispy and golden.

TOPPING
Try our *Tomato & Onion Relish* as a topping for a change. See recipe on page 261.

Peel the potatoes and cut lengthwise into strips about ⅜-inch (1cm) thick. Rinse under cold water and pat dry with a paper towel.

Fill a deep frying pan with enough oil to reach a depth of 3-inches (7.5 cm). Heat the oil over high heat.

Season the potato strips with salt.

Working in batches, drop the potatoes in the hot oil and fry until crispy and golden brown. Do not overcrowd the potatoes. Use a slotted spoon to remove the potatoes and place on a platter lined with paper towel to absorb the excess oil.

Serve immediately.

THERMOMETER
If using a thermometer, heat the oil over high heat until it registers 330°F (165°C). Do not heat the oil above 400°F (200°C) as it could smoke and burst into flames.

Red Roasted Potatoes

Mikres Kokkines Patates sto Fourno (Mee-KREHS KOH-kee-nehs Pah-TAH-tehs stoh FOOR-noh)

A blissfully simple and classy potato recipe with a touch of fragrant rosemary.

---

preparation 5 minutes   cooking 20 minutes   serves 4   bake 450°F (230°C)

Baby red potatoes, 1lb
(500g)
½ tsp salt
Pepper, as desired
2 tbsp fresh rosemary,
chopped
2 fresh rosemary sprigs
2 tbsp olive oil

Wash the potatoes and cut the larger ones in half so that all potatoes are roughly the same size.

Place in a roasting pan and season with salt and pepper.

Add the rosemary and drizzle with the olive oil.

Roast in the middle of a preheated oven for 20 minutes, or until the potatoes are fork tender.

Serve at once.

Cinnamon & Clove Potatoes

Patates me Kanella ke Yarifalo (Pah-TAH-tehs meh Kah-NEH-lah keh Yah-REE-fah-loh)

As children, our mother made us a potato soup with cinnamon and cloves. We have adapted that recipe into this potato side dish. We think it's a winner.

---

preparation 10 minutes   cooking 35 minutes   serves 4   bake 450°F (230°C)

---

8 yellow potatoes, 2lb
(1kg), peeled
¼ cup olive oil
2 tbsp tomato paste
½ cup warm water
1 ½ tsp salt
¼ tsp cloves, ground
¼ tsp cinnamon, ground
Pepper, as desired

Cut the peeled potatoes into wedges, roughly the same size so that they cook evenly. Place potatoes in a roasting pan with a fitted lid. Add the olive oil.

In a small cup dilute the tomato paste with the warm water and stir until the paste is diluted. Mix in the salt, cloves and cinnamon. Pour the ingredients into the roasting pan. Use a wooden spoon to mix the potatoes and coat them with the tomato sauce.

Top with fresh cracked pepper if desired.

Cook, covered, in a preheated over for 35 minutes or until the potatoes are fork tender. Half way through the cooking time, gently stir the potatoes to ensure they have an even coat of sauce.

Taste and adjust the seasonings if needed and serve.

Paprika Potatoes

Patates me Paprika (Pah-TAH-tehs meh Pah-PREE-kah)

A potato dish that is very versatile and popular with traditional Greek fare such as grilled meats and fish. Mildly flavoured but super tasty.

---

preparation 10 minutes   cooking 30 minutes   serves 4   bake 450°F (230°C)

---

8 yellow potatoes, 2lb
(1kg), peeled
1/3 cup olive oil
2 tbsp tomato paste
1 tsp salt
1 tsp paprika

Cut the peeled potatoes into wedges, roughly the same size so that they cook evenly. Place potatoes in a roasting pan. Add the remaining ingredients and toss lightly.

Place in the middle of a preheated oven for 30 minutes or until the potatoes are fork tender.

Taste and adjust the seasonings if needed and serve.

Lemon Potatoes

Patates me Lemoni (Pah-TAH-tehs meh Leh-MOH-nee)

Everyone loves lemon potatoes, whether on their own, with *Tsatziki*, with fish, or with grilled meat—the combinations are endless.

---

preparation 10 minutes   cooking 30 minutes   serves 4   bake 450°F (230°C)

---

8 yellow potatoes, 2lb
(1kg), peeled
1/3 cup olive oil
¼ cup lemon juice
1 tsp oregano, dried
1 tsp salt
Pepper, as desired

Cut the peeled potatoes into wedges, roughly the same size so that they cook evenly. Place potatoes in a roasting pan.

Whisk together the remaining ingredients and pour over the potatoes.

Place in the middle of a preheated oven for 30 minutes or until the potatoes are fork tender. Taste and adjust the seasonings if needed and serve.

"Food is not just a means for survival.

Cooking and eating can be one of the most sensuous and enjoyable aspects of your day."

Three Sisters—Betty, Eleni, Samantha

Cravings

Sweet Treats

Meze

Small Bites

Afternoon Coffee

This chapter excites us the most because we feel it holds some real gems that are yet undiscovered for many people.

Classy, yet simple to prepare, there isn't one on the list that all three of us don't love.

Main Dishes

Braised Chicken with Cinnamon & Cloves

Lemon Chicken & Potatoes

Santorini-Style Souvlaki on a Pita

Pork Medallions Stuffed with Sun-Dried Tomatoes & Goat Cheese

Pork & Celery Stew

Beef Tenderloin Stuffed with Figs & Apricots

Vegetables Stuffed with Onions, Beef & Rice

Braised Beef with Orzo

Roasted Leg of Lamb

Fresh Herb Crusted Rack of Lamb

Braised Rabbit with Pearl Onions

Baked Cod with a Tomato & Onion Relish

Salmon with Sun-Dried Tomatoes

Grilled Whole Red Snapper

Foil-wrapped Tilapia with Garlic Sauce

Poached Halibut with a Chickpea Tomato Sauce

Eggplant Slippers

Chickpea Burgers

Moussaka

Pasta with Eggplant & a Fresh Herb Tomato Sauce

Baked Penne Topped with Béchamel Sauce

Spaghetti with Sizzling Olive Oil & Mizithra

Braised Chicken with Cinnamon & Cloves

Kokkinisti Kota (Koh-kee-nee-STEE KOH-tah)

The smell of sautéed onions, cloves, cinnamon and nutmeg embracing tomatoes and chicken is divine. Absolutely mouth-watering, the aroma of this dish will fill your home and announce the meal to family and friends. This is the perfect dinner on a cold winter's day.

preparation 30 minutes   cooking 1 hour 30 minutes   serves 4

1 chicken, 3lb (1.5 kg)
½ tsp salt
¼ cup olive oil
1 yellow onion, minced
¼ tsp cinnamon, ground
or 1 cinnamon stick
5 cloves, whole
⅛ tsp nutmeg, ground
2 tbsp tomato paste
2 cups warm water
½ cup crushed tomato
sauce
1 lb (500g) egg noodles
or spaghetti, dried
½ cup Mizithra or
Pecorino Romano
cheese, grated

Prepare the whole chicken into serving pieces of roughly the same size. The breasts should be cut in two, the thighs should be separated from the legs and the wing tips should be removed and discarded. Remove the skin from the chicken pieces and discard. Salt the chicken pieces.

Heat the olive oil over high heat in a large pot with a fitted lid.

Reduce the heat and add the onion. Sauté until soft, about 5 minutes. Add the chicken to the pot and cook, about 2 minutes per side. The chicken will sweat and whiten as it cooks.

Add the cinnamon, cloves and nutmeg and give it a good stir.

In a cup dilute the tomato paste with the warm water and add it to the pot. Add the crushed tomato sauce.

Bring the ingredients to a boil and then reduce the heat. Simmer, partially covered, for at least 1 hour, until the chicken meat falls off the bone. If the chicken is not cooked all the way through continue simmering. The sauce should reduce and thicken. Taste and adjust the seasonings if needed.

In a separate pot cook the egg noodles. Place the cooked noodles on a plate and sprinkle with cheese. Top with pieces of chicken and thick cinnamon clove sauce. Serve at once.

Lemon Chicken & Potatoes

Kota me Patates sto Fourno (KOH-tah me Pah-TAH-tes sto FOOR-noh)

Lemon, oregano and olive oil, the triad at the heart of Greek cooking, infuses the potatoes and chicken in this heart-warming dish. This is a great fall back meal on a busy day, and it makes for an impressive meal for a dinner party too. The prep time is small but the taste is big! According to our dad, and he is right, the secret to this meal is the salt. A potato is only tasty if it has been married intimately with salt.

preparation 15 minutes   cooking 1 hour 30 minutes   serves 4   bake 425°F (220°C)

1 chicken, 4lb (2 kg)
8 yellow potatoes, 2lb (1kg) peeled and cut lengthwise into ½-inch (12mm) pieces
½ cup olive oil
¼ cup fresh lemon juice
2 tsp salt
1½ tsp oregano, dried
½ cup water
Pepper, as desired

TIP
This meal tastes best when a whole chicken is used. If using chicken pieces, ensure that they are bone-in, otherwise the chicken will become dry.

LEFTOVERS?
Save the leftovers and try *Leftover Lemon Chicken & Potato with Eggs*, on page 29, the next morning for breakfast.

Trim any excess fat from the chicken. Remove and discard the skin from the underside of the chicken. Place the chicken and the potatoes in a deep roasting pan with a fitted lid.

In a mixing bowl, whisk the olive oil and lemon juice. Pour over the chicken and the potatoes. Place the squeezed lemon halves in the chicken's body cavity.

Rub ½ teaspoon of salt on the chicken, and 1½ teaspoon salt on the potatoes. Rub the oregano over the potatoes and chicken.

Add ½ cup water to the roasting pan so that the potatoes are almost covered with liquid. Top the ingredients with some cracked pepper.

Place the roasting pan, covered, in a preheated oven for 1 hour 20 minutes. Continue cooking, uncovered for a further 10 minutes. The chicken leg should pull away from the body easily and the potatoes should be fork tender and golden. Taste and adjust the seasonings.

Serve warm.

Santorini-Style Souvlaki on a Pita

Souvlaki se Pita (Soov-LAH-kee seh PEE-tah)

Before the onset of the Euro, Greece was a haven for hungry backpackers. During that era, the three of us travelled to Greece and explored the islands. Our favourite was, and still is, the island of Santorini. This picturesque island is known for its blue-domed churches and white washed architecture. We fondly remember walking through the narrow, crowded streets of Fira, and heading toward one of several souvlaki stands. The souvlaki on a pita was always delicious and cost us next to nothing. Oh, the days of the drachma!

preparation 15 minutes   cooking 20 minutes   serves 6

Chicken breast, boneless, or pork tenderloin, 500g, cut into 1-inch (2.5cm) cubes
¼ tsp each salt & pepper
¼ tsp oregano, dried
Olive oil for drizzling

Fried Potatoes recipe, see page 139
Tsatziki recipe, see page 53
Lemon, Oregano & Olive Oil Dressing recipe, see page 262.

Olive oil for brushing
6 Greek-style pitas
1 Vidalia onion, diced
2 tomatoes, diced
Paprika
Cayenne pepper

WOODEN SKEWERS
Soak wooden skewers in cold water for 20 minutes before use.

Season the chicken or pork cubes with salt, pepper and oregano. Drizzle with olive oil and set aside.

Prepare the *Fried Potatoes, Tsatziki* and *Lemon, Oregano & Olive Oil Dressing* and set aside.

Thread the meat onto skewers. Place on a preheated grill over medium-high heat and cook for 4-6 minutes on each side or until the meat is completely cooked through. Chicken meat should be white on the inside, and the pork should be pink.

Remove the meat from the skewers and place in a bowl. Toss with the *Lemon, Oregano & Olive Oil Dressing*.

Lightly brush the pitas with olive oil and place on the grill, oil side down over low heat. Remove from grill once pita is warmed on both sides.

Lay a piece of wax paper on the counter. Place 3/4 of the pita on the wax paper. Arrange generous amounts of meat, *Fried Potatoes, Tsatziki*, onions and tomatoes on the pita. Sprinkle with paprika and cayenne pepper.

Fold the pita in half and tightly wrap the wax paper around the pita. Twist the wax paper at the bottom so that the dressings do not fall out and serve.

Pork Medallions Stuffed with Sun-Dried Tomatoes & Goat Cheese

Hirino me Domates ke Tiri (Hee-ree-NOH meh doh-MAH-tes keh tee-REE)

Easy to prepare and beautiful to serve—this pork dish is a hit. Creamy goat cheese and salty flavourful sun-dried tomatoes fill the centre of a seasoned pork tenderloin. Need we say more?

---

preparation 10 minutes   cooking 20 minutes   serves 2-4   bake 425°F (220°C)

---

1 pork tenderloin, 1½ lb (750g)
¼ tsp each salt & pepper
1 tsp oregano, dried
1/3 cup sun-dried tomatoes packed in oil, chopped
1 garlic clove, minced
2 tbsp each fresh basil & fresh parsley, minced
1/3 cup goat cheese, crumbled
3 uncooked spaghetti noodles
2 tbsp olive oil

MAKE AHEAD
The tenderloin can be stuffed, wrapped in plastic and refrigerated on the morning of serving day.

VARIATIONS
Try changing the filling with different herbs, dried fruits and cheeses. E.g. rosemary, cranberry & feta cheese.

Trim away the excess fat and silver skin from the tenderloin. Prepare the tenderloin for stuffing by slicing the tenderloin lengthwise almost all the way through. Open it up like a book. Cut through each half almost all the way through again and pound to flatten, ½-inch (12mm) thick. Season the inside of the pork with salt, pepper and oregano.

Prepare the stuffing ingredients by combining the sun-dried tomatoes, garlic, herbs and cheese in a small bowl. Spread the stuffing on the entire surface of the flattened tenderloin. Tightly roll up the pork so that it is shaped like a tenderloin once again and resembles a spiral.

Break up the uncooked spaghetti noodles into 2-inch (5cm) pieces and pierce them through the tenderloin to hold it together and keep the stuffing inside.

Heat the oil in an ovenproof skillet over high heat. Use tongs to place the tenderloin in the heated skillet. Ensure that the skillet is large enough to hold the tenderloin securely as the oil will splatter if the skillet is too big. Sear the pork tenderloin until it is lightly browned on all sides, about 2 minutes per side.

Remove the skillet from the stove-top and place directly in the upper third of the preheated oven for 20 minutes. Ensure that the pork is seam upright.

Transfer the pork to a cutting board and cover with foil for 5 minutes. Slice the pork into medallions. Remove any bits of pasta that are noticeable before serving.

Pork & Celery Stew

Fricassee apo Hirino ke Selino (Free-kah-SEH ah-POH Hee-ree-NOH keh SEH-lee-noh)

When our mom made this stew, her pot was reminiscent of a magician's hat. The pot would be full of greens, and then another colander full would be added, and still a third colander would be added. Magically the greens would reduce in volume and turn into the perfect one-pot stew. Tradition calls for lots of celery, lettuce, and escarole. This unique dish is silky, creamy and comforting. Serve with fresh bread.

preparation 15 minutes   cooking 60 minutes   serves 4

1 rib-end pork loin, French trimmed, 1 ½ lb (750 g)
Salt
2 tbsp olive oil
1 yellow onion, minced
8 celery stalks and leaves, thinly chopped
1 tsp salt
3 cups water
1 red leaf lettuce, &
1 endive escarole, 1 lb (500g) total of greens

Lemon & Egg Sauce recipe, see page 260

MAKE AHEAD
The stew can be made the morning of serving day and reheated prior to the preparation of the Lemon & Egg Sauce.

Using a sharp knife, cut the pork along the bone into serving pieces. Sprinkle with salt and set aside.

Heat the oil in a large pot over medium heat. Add the onion and sauté for 5 minutes. Add the pork and cook for 2 minutes on each side until the pork is slightly browned on both sides.

Add the celery, salt and 3 cups water. Bring to a boil and reduce the heat. Simmer, covered, for 30-45 minutes until the celery is soft.

Cut out the center core of both the lettuce and escarole. Wash the greens thoroughly. Chop the greens coarsely into 1-inch (2.5cm) pieces. Place in a salad spinner to remove excess water. Add the lettuce and endive escarole a bit at a time to the pot. The greens will significantly reduce in volume when cooked. Simmer, covered, for a further 20 minutes.

Prepare the *Lemon & Egg Sauce*. Add the sauce to the pot and heat through over medium heat.

Serve immediately.

Beef Tenderloin Stuffed with Figs & Apricots

Moshari me Sika ke Verikoka (Mohs-HAH-ree meh SEE-kah keh Veh-REE-koh-kah)

This recipe makes for a very impressive formal dinner. A whole beef tenderloin is stuffed with sautéed dried apricots, dried figs, walnuts, shallots, garlic and rosemary. Once the tenderloin has cooked, it is served with a sauce of fresh figs and apricots instead of dried ones. The combination of dried and fresh fruit, the smell of garlic, wine, and rosemary—it is all just heavenly.

preparation 60 minutes   cooking 20 minutes   serves 6   bake 350°F (180°C)

½ cup dried figs
½ cup dried apricots
2 tbsp olive oil
2 shallots, minced
¼ cup fresh rosemary, chopped
½ cup white wine
2 tbsp walnuts, ground
1 beef tenderloin, 2½ lb (1.25kg)
2 garlic cloves, minced
1 tsp salt
Pepper, as desired
2 tbsp olive oil

FOR THE SAUCE
2 tbsp olive oil
2 shallots, minced
2 tbsp fresh rosemary, chopped
½ cup red wine
1 cup beef broth
6 apricots, sliced
6 Black Mission or Kalamata figs, quartered

MAKE AHEAD
The tenderloin can be stuffed, wrapped in plastic and refrigerated on the morning of serving day.

Place the dried figs and apricots in a small saucepan with 2 cups boiling water. Set aside for 20 minutes until the fruit has softened. Once soft, chop the fruit and set aside.

Heat the olive oil in a saucepan over medium heat. Add the shallots and cook until soft. Add 2 tablespoons of the rosemary to the saucepan along with the white wine. Bring to a boil, and reduce the wine by half. Add the chopped figs and apricots set aside earlier to the pan and cook until all of the wine has evaporated. Remove the pan from the heat and add the ground walnuts. Transfer to a small bowl and set aside to cool.

Use a sharp knife to remove the fat and silvery skin from the beef tenderloin. Cut the tenderloin through the middle lengthwise and stop at about 3/4-inch (2cm) from the other side. Open up the tenderloin and arrange an even layer of the cooled stuffing on the one side. Close up the tenderloin and tie the tenderloin securely with kitchen string. Use about three to four strings and space them apart in equal lengths. Trim away the excess string.

Spread the garlic, the remaining 2 tablespoons rosemary, salt and pepper on a cutting board. Roll the tenderloin over the ingredients until the tenderloin is evenly coated. Wrap tightly with plastic wrap and place in the refrigerator.

To prepare the sauce, heat the olive oil in a large sauté pan over high heat. Add the shallots and rosemary and sauté for 2 minutes. Add the red wine and reduce by half. Add the broth and fresh fruit and bring to a boil.

Reduce the heat and simmer for 20 minutes until the sauce has thickened. Set aside.

Meanwhile, remove the tenderloin from the refrigerator and discard the plastic wrap. Heat the oil in a large ovenproof skillet over high heat. The skillet should be large enough to hold the tenderloin securely. When the oil is hot, add the tenderloin and sear on all sides until brown, about 2 minutes per side.

Place the skillet in the middle of a preheated oven and bake for 20 minutes. Remove from the oven and transfer the tenderloin to a cutting board. Cover the tenderloin with foil and let it rest for 5 minutes.

Cut the tenderloin into 1-inch (2.5cm) pieces. Arrange the pieces on a serving platter and top with sauce. Serve immediately.

Vegetables Stuffed with Onions, Beef & Rice

Yemista (Yeh-mee-STAH)

There are many variations to stuffed vegetables; this one is similar to our stuffed tomato recipe. The addition of beef makes these vegetables heartier and definitely pleases the carnivores in the family. Serve with feta cheese and some plain Greek or Balkan style yogurt.

preparation 35 minutes   cooking 60 minutes   serves 6   bake 425°F (220°C)

6 tomatoes, whole
4 peppers, whole
1lb (500g) ground beef, extra lean
2 yellow onions, minced
1½ tsp salt
1 tsp oregano, dried
½ cup white wine
½ cup crushed tomato sauce
1 cup Arborio rice
½ cup fresh mint, chopped
½ cup olive oil
Pepper, as desired
6 potatoes, peeled, cut lengthwise into 1-inch (2.5cm) pieces
½ tsp salt

Using a sharp tomato knife, slice off the tops of the tomatoes to make a lid. If possible, try not to cut the lid off completely. Remove the tough inner core of the tomato. Scoop the soft flesh of the tomatoes with a spoon and place in a large bowl. Break up any large pieces of tomato flesh with your hands.

Make lids for the peppers and seed them. Place the hollowed vegetables in a large roasting pan with a fitted lid. The pan should be large enough to hold the vegetables securely with enough room for the potatoes.

Sauté the ground beef in a large saucepan over medium heat. Drain the fat if needed.

Add the onions, salt and oregano. Cook until the onions are soft, about 5 minutes.

Add the wine and cook until reduced by half. Add the tomato flesh set aside earlier and heat through along with the crushed tomato sauce.

Add the rice, and simmer for 15 minutes over low heat so that the rice is parboiled. Stir in the mint, ¼ cup of the olive oil and some fresh cracked pepper.

Fill the tomatoes and peppers with the beef and rice mixture and place the lids on the vegetables.

Lightly salt the potatoes and place in the roasting pan around the stuffed vegetables.

Drizzle the remaining olive oil in the roasting pan and place in the middle of a preheated oven, covered, for 50 minutes. Remove the lid and cook for 10 minutes further. The vegetables will release juices while in the oven, this will help cook the rice.

Remove the roasting pan from the oven and let it stand for 10 minutes before serving.

MAKE AHEAD
Two hours before baking you can prepare the beef and rice mixture. Set it aside at room temperature and stuff the vegetables just before you are ready to place in the oven. The potatoes can also be peeled and immersed in water until ready to cook.

Braised Beef with Orzo

Youvetsi (Yoo-VEH-tsee)

This is a sublime dish: warm, velvety and comforting. Orzo, a barley-shaped pasta, cooks alongside beef in a fragrant and mild tomato sauce. After baking in the oven it is topped with Kefalotiri, a salty cheese, and served. So, so yummy.

---

preparation 10 minutes   cooking 2 hours 40 minutes   serves 8   bake 400°F (200°C)

---

1 eye of round roast, 3lb
(1.5kg)
2/3 cup olive oil
1 yellow onion, chopped
1½ tsp salt
Pepper, as desired
¼ cup white wine
2 tbsp tomato paste
8 cloves
1 cup hot water
3 cups Greek orzo, dried
8 cups boiling water
Mizithra, kefalotiri or
Pecorino Romano
cheese, grated

ORZO
Greek orzo takes longer to cook than Italian orzo and retains a firmer consistency when cooked. Quantities of water and cooking times must be adjusted accordingly if Greek orzo is not used.

Remove the excess fat from the beef roast using a sharp knife. Cut the roast into 1-inch (2.5cm) slices. Place in a large bowl and immerse the beef in boiling water for 2 minutes. Drain.

Transfer the meat to a cutting board and cut each slice into 2 or 3 pieces so that all pieces are roughly the same size.

In a large sauté pan, heat the oil over medium-high heat. Add the onion and sauté for 2-3 minutes. Add the beef, salt and pepper and sauté for 3-4 minutes. The beef will release juices. Add the white wine and cook for 1 minute. Add the tomato paste, cloves and 1 cup hot water. Let the ingredients heat through. Simmer, partially covered for 2 hours until the meat is tender and the sauce has reduced.

Transfer the beef and sauce to a large roasting pan. Add the orzo and 8 cups boiling water. Place in the middle of a preheated oven for 30-40 minutes until the orzo is soft and cooked through.

Serve immediately and top with cheese.

Roasted Leg of Lamb

Arnisto Fourno (Ahr-NEE stoh FOOR-noh)

Growing up in Toronto's Greek town meant the sight of lambs hanging in butcher shops was common at Easter time. Our family would always purchase a whole lamb to be cooked on a spit on our front lawn. The sight of the skewered lamb was shocking and memorable to say the least. It cooked for hours on end while we played and the adults danced.

Skewering and cooking a whole lamb is not for the light-hearted. More and more, families roast only a leg of lamb at Easter time. The smell of the lamb cooking infuses homes rather than the outdoors, nevertheless the feast is just as delicious.

---

preparation 15 minutes   cooking 2 hours   serves 6   roast 325°F (165°C)

---

1 leg of lamb, 4lb (2kg)
4 garlic cloves, sliced
Juice of ½ lemon
Olive oil for coating
1 tbsp oregano, dried
1 tsp salt
1 tsp pepper

HOW TO CARVE A LEG OF LAMB
Use a towel to hold the bone securely in your hands. Turn the lamb so that the meat side is up. In your other hand hold a sharp carving knife and cut the lamb in a downwards fashion away from your body. Keep the slices ½-inch (12mm) thick. Ensure that you carve around the bone.

Remove the excess fat from the lamb using a sharp kitchen knife.

Cut slits, ½-inch (12mm) deep, into the meaty surface of the lamb and insert a slice of garlic in each opening. Squeeze the lemon juice over the lamb and lightly coat with olive oil.

In a small mixing bowl, combine the oregano, salt and pepper. Season the lamb with the mix. Place the leg of lamb in a shallow roasting pan just large enough to hold it securely. Lay the lamb in the pan round side up. Insert a meat thermometer into the thickest part of the lamb away from the bone, and place the pan in the middle of the preheated oven.

For medium-rare, roast the lamb for a minimum of 1 ½ hours. It will need to cook at least 30 minutes longer for a medium to well-done roast. Let your meat thermometer be your guide!

Transfer the lamb from the oven to the counter and tent it with foil for 20 minutes. Keep in mind that the lamb continues to cook during this time, 10-15 degrees. Place the lamb on a cutting board, carve and serve.

MAKE AHEAD
The lamb can be seasoned and refrigerated one day in advance. Let it sit at room temperature for 1 hour before placing in the oven.

Fresh Herb-Crusted Rack of Lamb

Arni me Fresca Votana (Ahr-NEE meh FREHS-kah VOH-tah-nah)

A very elegant main dish or a great starter. Serve the ribs individually and offer *Tsatziki* as a dip.

---

preparation 15 minutes   cooking 20 minutes   serves 4   roast 450°F (230°C)

---

2 racks of lamb, 1½ lb (750g), 7 or 8 ribs each
2 garlic cloves, sliced
¼ cup each fresh parsley, mint, basil, minced
Olive oil for coating
¼ tsp each salt & pepper

Tsatziki dip, see recipe page 53

MAKE AHEAD
The lamb racks can be prepared the morning of serving day and refrigerated until they are ready to be seared.

Trim away the fat from the lamb racks. Cut each rack in half so that there are 3 or 4 ribs in each piece.

Cut slits, ½-inch (12mm) deep, into the meaty side of the lamb and insert a slice of garlic in each opening.

Combine the herbs in a bowl and set aside.

Brush the lamb with olive oil and season with salt and pepper. Heat a heavy ovenproof frying pan over high heat. The size of the pan should be large enough to hold the lamb racks comfortably. Sear both sides of the lamb, about 2 minutes per side. Remove the pan from the heat and transfer the lamb to a cutting board.

Generously cover the meaty side of the lamb with the fresh herbs set aside earlier. Place the lamb back in the ovenproof pan and place in the middle of a preheated oven. Cook 15 minutes for medium, or 18 minutes for well-done.

Remove the lamb from the pan. Cover it with foil and let it rest for 15 minutes. Keep in mind that the lamb will continue to cook during this time.

Carve the lamb racks into single chops and arrange on a serving platter. Serve at once with *Tsatziki* for dipping.

Braised Rabbit with Pearl Onions

Stifado (Stee-FAH-doh)

Peasant men hunted for dinner and women dreamed up of ways to prepare the coming meal. It was surely the scarcity of ingredients in a winter pantry that led to the creation of this sweet onion stew. If the thought of eating rabbit does not interest you, then you will be happy to know this recipe works just as well with other game such as venison or pheasant, but even stewing beef make for delicious variations. This is a fragrant and elegant dinner.

---

preparation 30 minutes   cooking 2 hours   serves 4

---

1 rabbit, 3lb (1.5kg), cut into serving pieces
1½ tsp salt
¼ cup olive oil
3 tbsp tomato paste
1 cup Mavrodaphne, or other dessert wine
2 bay leaves
4 garlic cloves, chopped
1 cinnamon stick
1 tsp sweet paprika
8 cloves, whole
¼ tsp pepper
1½ cups water
4 cups red pearl onions

HOW TO PEEL PEARL ONIONS
Place them in a pot of boiling water for 3 minutes. Remove the onions from the water and let them cool. Cut the tips off and squeeze until the onion pops away from the skin.

Sprinkle the rabbit pieces with ½ teaspoon salt. In a large pot heat the oil over high heat. Add the rabbit pieces and sear on all sides, about 2 minutes per side. This will seal in the juices and keep the rabbit tender. If needed, brown the rabbit in batches. Overcrowding meat causes it to steam.

Add the tomato paste, Mavrodaphne and give it a good stir.

Add the bay leaves, garlic, cinnamon, paprika, cloves, and the remaining salt and pepper.

Pour in 1½ cups water and bring to a boil. Reduce the heat and simmer, partially covered for 1 hour and 15 minutes.

Meanwhile peel the pearl onions.

Add the pearl onions to the pot and continue simmering for 30-45 minutes further until the rabbit is cooked through and the onions are tender enough to melt in your mouth. Discard the bay leaves before serving.

Serve warm with fresh bread and *Fried Potatoes* if desired.

SUBSTITUTION
If using stewing beef, reduce the amount to 1½lb (750g).

MAVRODAPHNE In remote Greek villages, *Stifado* is made with red wine vinegar. This changes the flavour of the dish but it is still very enjoyable and unique. We recommend using Mavrodaphne because it imparts a richer flavour and is fragrant. Mavrodaphne is a dark, sweet dessert wine. To Orthodox Christians, the taste of this wine will be strongly associated with communion. If you have difficulty locating Mavrodaphne, any good quality dessert wine is acceptable.

Baked Cod with a Tomato & Onion Relish

Vakalaos me Salsa Domatas ke Kremidi (Vah-kah-LAH-ohs meh SAHL-sah Doh-MAH-tahs keh Kreh-MEE-dee)

Salted cod is very popular in Greece. It is soaked in water for days to remove the excess salt and then battered and deep fried. In our opinion, baking or grilling cod is just as delicious. It's up to you—both options are yummy.

preparation 5 minutes   cooking 15 minutes   serves 4   bake 400°F (200°C)

Tomato & Onion Relish recipe, see page 261.

4 cod fillets, 12oz (375g) each, about 1-inch (2.5cm) thick, washed & patted dry
¼ tsp each salt & pepper
¼ cup white wine or water

Prepare the *Tomato & Onion Relish*.

Arrange the cod fillets in a shallow baking dish. Season with salt and pepper. Pour the wine into the pan. This prevents the fish from sticking to the bottom of the pan.

Place the cod in the middle of a preheated oven for 12-15 minutes, or until the flesh is opaque and the thickest part of the cod flakes when pierced with a fork.

Remove the cod from the oven and transfer to a serving platter. Generously top the cod with the *Tomato & Onion Relish* and serve immediately.

Salmon with Sun-Dried Tomatoes

Solomos me Steynes Domates (Soh-loh-MOHS meh Stehy-NEHS Doh-MAH-tehs)

Salmon topped with sun-dried tomatoes and feta cheese looks beautiful and tastes delicious. A great choice anytime.

---

preparation 10 minutes   cooking 15 minutes   serves 4   bake 450°F (230°C)

---

4 salmon fillets, 8oz (250g) each, rinsed and patted dry
Pepper as desired
1 cup sun-dried tomatoes, packed in oil, chopped
½ cup feta cheese, crumbled
3 garlic cloves, minced

Season the salmon with pepper.

Combine the sun-dried tomatoes, feta cheese and garlic in a small bowl.

Place the salmon on a lightly greased baking sheet and top each fillet with a generous amount of the mixture.

Place the salmon in the middle of a preheated oven and bake for 12-15 minutes, or until the thickest part of the salmon flakes when pierced with a fork. Serve.

Grilled Whole Red Snapper

Psari sti Shara (PSAH-ree stee SHA-rah)

Serving a fish whole is very impressive and not difficult at all. Pick a nice hot day, grill some fish, drizzle it with some *Lemon, Oregano and Olive Oil Dressing* and let yourself get transported to a beach front restaurant in the south of Greece!

---

preparation 5 minutes   cooking 15 minutes   serves 4

---

2 whole red snapper, 1lb (500g), scaled & gutted
4 sprigs fresh oregano
4 lemon slices
Olive oil for coating
Salt & pepper

Lemon, Oregano & Olive Oil Dressing, see recipe page 262.

GRILL BASKETS
Using a grill basket makes grilling fish much easier. Ensure that the basket is well greased before placing the fish inside.

Rinse the fish and lightly pat dry. Stuff the inside of the fish with the fresh oregano and lemon slices. Coat the fish lightly with olive oil and season with salt and pepper.

Prepare the *Lemon, Oregano & Olive Oil Dressing*.

Place the fish directly on a preheated grill over medium heat. Grill for 6 minutes per side or until the fish is cooked through.

Remove the fish from the grill and arrange on a cutting board. Carefully open the fish fillets by cutting the top side of the fish with a sharp knife below the gills, along the belly towards the tail and up. Open the fillet and carefully remove the bones. Transfer the fish fillets to serving plates.

Drizzle the *Lemon, Oregano & Olive Oil Dressing* on the fillets and serve.

Foil-Wrapped Tilapia with Garlic Sauce

Psari stí Shara me Salsa Skordou (PSAH-ree stee SHA-rah meh SAHL-sah SKOR-doo)

White fish tends to be easily interchangeable so this recipe also works well with sea bass and cod. The fish can be wrapped in foil and grilled, or simply grilled in a basket. When cooked, top it with this delicious garlic sauce. It is reminiscent of a sauce we tried in Cyprus once. With only our memory and culinary ingenuity, we have recreated it. We may have even improved it!

preparation 15 minutes   cooking 10 minutes   serves 4

8 garlic cloves, whole, unpeeled
1 shallot, minced
1 cup white wine, chardonnay
2 tbsp tomato paste
3 tbsp heavy cream, 18%
1 tsp brown sugar
Pinch of salt
Pepper as desired
4 tilapia fillets, 7oz (200g) each
Olive oil for coating
Salt & pepper

Toss the garlic in a small frying pan over high heat. Remove from the heat when the garlic has blackened on both sides. This gives the garlic a smoky flavour. Set aside.

In a small saucepan, add the shallot and white wine over high heat. Maintain a steady boil until the wine has reduced by half.

Reduce the heat and stir in the tomato paste, heavy cream and brown sugar. Once the sauce is warmed through, remove it from the heat and transfer it to a food processor.

Peel the skins off of the blackened garlic cloves. Add them to the food processor and purée. Place the sauce back in the saucepan, add a pinch of salt and pepper to taste and simmer over low heat for 10 minutes. Keep warm.

Lay the tilapia on a large piece of foil. Lightly coat the tilapia with olive oil and season with salt and pepper. Lay another sheet of foil on top of the fish and fold over the edges tightly to seal the fish.

Place the foil-wrapped tilapia directly on a grill rack over medium heat. Grill for 10 minutes or until the flesh is flaky and pulls apart easily when pierced with a fork.

Remove the tilapia from the grill and discard the foil. Arrange on serving plates. Top generously with the garlic sauce and serve.

Poached Halibut with a Chickpea Tomato Sauce

Psari me Revithia ke Domata Salsa (PSAH-ree meh Reh-VEE-thee-ah keh Doh-MAH-tah SAHL-sah)

In this recipe, halibut, a mild flavoured white fish, is poached in a tomato sauce infused with wine, olives, capers and chickpeas. This dish is beautiful to behold and healthy! Cod, tilapia, red snapper, mahi mahi or even swordfish can be substituted.

---

preparation 10 minutes   cooking 20 minutes   serves 4

---

2 tbsp olive oil
2 shallots, minced
2 garlic cloves, minced
½ cup white wine
4 tomatoes, diced
1 tsp salt
1 cup chickpeas, cooked
¼ cup Kalamata olives, pits removed, chopped
3 tsp capers
1 tsp red pepper flakes (optional)
Pepper, as desired
4 halibut steaks, 12oz (375g) each, about 1-inch (2.5cm) thick
¼ cup fresh parsley, chopped

Heat the olive oil in a large deep skillet over medium heat. Add the shallots and sauté for 3 minutes. Add the garlic and sauté for 1 minute. Add the wine and reduce by half. Add the tomatoes and salt and heat through, about 2 minutes. Add the chickpeas, olives, capers, and red pepper flakes if desired. Grind some pepper and cook for about 5 minutes.

Nestle the halibut steaks in the chickpea tomato sauce. Do not overlap the halibut steaks. Spoon the sauce over the fish. Cook for 6-8 minutes or until the halibut flesh is flaky and pulls apart easily when pierced with a fork.

Remove the pan from the heat, stir in the parsley and serve.

MAKE AHEAD
The cooled sauce can be stored in an airtight container and refrigerated for up to 2 days. Gently reheat the sauce before adding the fish.

Eggplant Slippers

Pappoutsakia (Pah-poo-TSAH-kee-ah)

This dish is simple to prepare, especially if the meat sauce has been made ahead of time. The remaining prep consists of topping halved eggplants with sauce, tomatoes and cheese. So cute and impressive. Béchamel can be used in place of the cheese topping for a more traditional variation.

preparation 55 minutes   cooking 20 minutes   serves 6 main or 12 side   roast 350°F (180°C) & bake 400°F (200°C)

Meat Sauce recipe, see page 258

6 small eggplants
Salt
Olive oil for greasing
½ cup goat cheese
½ cup feta cheese, crumbled
1 tomato, sliced
Pepper as desired

MAKE AHEAD
The *Meat Sauce* can be made up to 2 days in advance and refrigerated or it can be kept in the freezer for up to 4 months.

Prepare the *Meat Sauce* and set aside.

Slice the eggplants in half lengthways and sprinkle with salt. Set aside for 20 minutes so that the salt can draw out the bitter juices. Pat dry with a paper towel.

Place the eggplants flesh side down on a greased baking sheet. Place in the middle of a preheated oven and roast for 35 minutes or until the eggplant is brown and soft all the way through. Meanwhile, mix the goat cheese and crumbled feta in a bowl and set aside.

Remove the eggplants from oven, use a spatula to carefully turn them over. Score the eggplant flesh into small squares using a sharp kitchen knife.

Top the scored eggplants with some meat sauce, sliced tomatoes, and cheese. Season with fresh cracked pepper. Place in the middle of a preheated oven and bake for 20 minutes until the tomatoes have softened and the cheese has melted.

Serve.

Chickpea Burgers

Revithokeftedes (Reh-vee-tho-kehf-TEH-dehs)

This is a foolproof recipe for great tasting vegetarian burgers. They have a complex flavour from the combination of sautéed onions, red peppers, herbs and spices. Simply delicious.
If you are making these burgers for young children, you may want to modify the amount of spices or onions used.

preparation 10 minutes   cooking 25 minutes   makes 10-12 patties   convection bake 400°F (200°C)

2 tbsp olive oil
1 yellow onion, diced
2 cups chickpeas, cooked
1 red pepper, deseeded, quartered
2 garlic cloves, sliced
1 carrot, chopped
1¼ cup fresh bread crumbs
1 tsp salt
½ tsp cumin, ground
¼ tsp coriander, ground
½ cup fresh parsley, minced
Olive oil for coating

CONVECTION BAKING
With convection baking you omit the step of having to flip ingredients over to brown them on both sides. If you do not have a convection oven then you will need to cook the patties for 10 minutes on one side and then flip and cook for another 10 minutes.

Heat the olive oil in a small sauté pan over medium heat. Add the onions and sauté until soft, about 5 minutes. Transfer to a large bowl and let cool.

Place the chickpeas, red pepper, garlic, and carrot in a food processor and pulse until all of the ingredients are blended. Transfer to the large bowl with the onions. Add the remaining ingredients to the bowl and use your hands to combine the ingredients.

Shape the mixture into patties and use a brush to lightly grease both sides of the patties with olive oil.

Transfer the patties to a baking sheet and place in the middle of a preheated oven for 20 minutes or until the patties are golden-brown on both sides.

Use a spatula to remove the patties from the baking sheet. Serve on a bun with your favourite garnishes: pickles, tomatoes, lettuce, red onions, the possibilities are endless!

MAKE AHEAD
The chickpea mixture can be prepared on the morning of serving day and stored in the refrigerator until ready to shape into patties.

TIP
Make your own bread crumbs for this recipe by placing 2 slices of bread in a food processor.

Moussaka

(Moo-sah-KAH)

This version of Moussaka is a true Greek classic. It consists of eggplant, zucchini, potatoes, meat sauce, Béchamel and aromatic nutmeg and cinnamon. To make this dish lighter, we broil the vegetables instead of frying them for a version that is hearty and delicious but less heavy. If you dislike eggplant (though we can't imagine why) simply omit and add more zucchini.

preparation 40 minutes	cooking 35 minutes	serves 6	broil 500°F (260°C) & bake 350°F (180°C)

Meat Sauce recipe, see page 258

1 eggplant, sliced, ¼ inch (6mm) thick
Salt
3 zucchini, sliced, ¼-inch (6mm) thick
4 potatoes, sliced, ¼-inch (6mm) thick
Olive oil for brushing
Salt

Béchamel Sauce recipe, see page 259

¼ tsp nutmeg, ground
¼ tsp cinnamon, ground

MAKE AHEAD
The Meat Sauce can be made up to 2 days in advance and refrigerated or it can be kept in the freezer for up to 4 months.
The Béchamel Sauce can be made up to 2 days in advance and refrigerated.

Prepare the Meat Sauce and set aside.

Lightly salt the eggplants slices. Set aside for 20 minutes so that the salt can draw out the bitter juices. Pat dry with a paper towel.

Lightly brush both sides of the eggplant, zucchini and potatoes with olive oil. Sprinkle the vegetables with salt and arrange on a baking sheet. Place in a preheated oven and broil until lightly golden on both sides. Set aside.

Pour a thin layer of meat sauce in the bottom of a 9x12-inch (23x30cm) pan. Arrange the potatoes in an even layer in the pan followed by the zucchini and eggplant. Top each vegetable layer with some meat sauce.

Prepare the Béchamel Sauce.

Top the Moussaka with an even layer of Béchamel sauce. Sprinkle with nutmeg and cinnamon and place in a preheated oven for 35 minutes, or until lightly browned.

Let the dish sit for 10 minutes at room temperature before cutting and serving to allow the Béchamel Sauce to firm.

VARIATION
Turn this into a vegetarian meal by omitting the meat sauce and adding your favourite tomato sauce instead.
Use our Fresh Tomato Sauce recipe on page 257.

Pasta with Eggplant & a Fresh Herb Tomato Sauce

Pasta me Fresca Votana (PAH-stah meh FREHS-kah VOH-tah-nah)

This dish is a salute to summer and all the goodness of a simple garden with tomatoes and fresh herbs such as parsley, mint, basil and oregano. Eggplant is treated like an edible garnish, and yogurt adds a refreshing twist.

preparation 20 minutes   cooking 40 minutes   serves 4   broil 500°F (260°C)

1 eggplant, sliced
¼-inch (6mm) thick
Salt
Olive oil for brushing
2 tbsp olive oil
5 scallions, chopped,
both white and green
2 garlic cloves, pressed
6 plum tomatoes,
deseeded, chopped
1 tsp salt
¼ cup each, fresh
parsley & basil, chopped
1 tbsp each fresh mint &
oregano, chopped
Pepper, as desired
12oz (375g) spaghetti or
penne pasta, dried
Mizithra or Pecorino
Romano cheese, grated
Dollops of yogurt, Greek
or Balkan style

Arrange the eggplant slices on a baking sheet. Lightly salt and set aside for 20 minutes. Pat the eggplant dry with paper towel to absorb the bitter juices that have been released. Lightly brush both sides of the eggplant with olive oil and place in the middle of a preheated oven. Broil until lightly golden on both sides, about 10 minutes per side. Remove from broiler and set aside.

Heat the olive oil in a medium saucepan over high heat. Lower the heat and add the scallions. Sauté until soft. Add the garlic and sauté for 1 minute.

Add the tomatoes and salt and sauté until the tomatoes have released their juices and reabsorbed them, about 10 minutes.

Stir in the fresh herbs, season with pepper and remove from the heat.

Bring a large pot of salted water to boil. Cook the pasta to your liking.

Arrange the eggplant slices on individual serving plates. Top with pasta and a sprinkle of cheese. Add a scoop of the fresh herb tomato sauce and finish with a dollop of yogurt. Serve at once.

Baked Penne topped with Béchamel Sauce

Pastitsio (Pah-STEE-tsee-oh)

Pastitsio never fails to please. Kids love it, adults love it—it's a crowd favourite. Pastitsio is to Greeks what lasagna is to Italians. It is a dish Greek moms will always bring to a get together. Unashamedly rich, creamy, and aromatic, it is well worth the effort involved in putting it together.

---

preparation 15 minutes   cooking 35 minutes   serves 6   bake 400°F (200°C)

Meat Sauce recipe,
see page 258

5 cups penne regate
pasta, dried
¼ cup Mizithra or
Pecorino Romano
cheese, grated

Béchamel Sauce recipe,
see page 259

2 tbsp Mizithra or
Pecorino Romano
cheese, grated
6 slivers of butter
¼ tsp cinnamon
¼ tsp nutmeg

MAKE AHEAD
The Meat Sauce can be made up to 2 days in advance and refrigerated or it can be kept in the freezer for up to 4 months.
The Béchamel Sauce can be made up to 2 days in advance and refrigerated.

Prepare the *Meat Sauce*. Set aside.

Bring a large pot of salted water to boil and cook the penne pasta to your liking.

Place the cooked penne in a large rectangular baking dish, 11x14-inch (28x35cm), and sprinkle with cheese.

Pour the *Meat Sauce* on top of the penne pasta and mix it together so that the penne is evenly coated with sauce.

Prepare the *Béchamel Sauce*. Spread the Béchamel sauce evenly on top of the pasta and meat sauce.

Top the *Béchamel Sauce* with cheese and slivers of butter. Sprinkle with cinnamon and nutmeg and place directly in a preheated oven for 35 minutes, or until lightly browned.

Let the dish sit for 10 minutes on the counter before cutting and serving to allow the *Béchamel Sauce* to firm.

Spaghetti with Sizzling Olive Oil & Mizithra

Pasta me Mizithra ke Kafto Ladi (PAH-stah meh Mee-DZEE-thrah keh Kaf-TOH LAH-dee)

Our dad used to make this Greek version of spaghetti and cheese for us when we were kids. It is still a family favourite. He would heat up olive oil in a small frying pan, drop individual swirls of pasta into the hot oil and fry them until they were crispy and golden brown. This crispy noodle crown would top a plate of spaghetti that had been tossed with Mizithra cheese. A drizzle of the remaining hot olive oil finished off the dish.

---

preparation 15 minutes   cooking 20 minutes   serves 4

1kg (500g) spaghetti, cooked
Mizithra or Pecorino Romano cheese, grated
1/3 cup olive oil

Toss the cooked spaghetti with as much cheese as desired.

Arrange the spaghetti in four pasta bowls.

Heat the olive oil in a frying pan over medium-high heat. Gather 4-5 spaghetti noodles from a pasta bowl and drop it in the hot oil. Cook until crispy and brown on one side. Carefully flip and fry the spaghetti until brown on the other side. Use a slotted spoon to transfer the noodle crown on top of a pasta bowl.

Repeat with the other bowls of pasta.

Pour spoonfuls of hot oil on top of each pasta bowl and serve immediately.

Desserts in Greek culture are not limited to after-dinner indulgences. In fact, they are mostly enjoyed with an afternoon coffee, making the break in the middle of the day just a little sweeter!

Desserts

Braided Cookies
Almond Butter Cookies
Honey-Dipped Walnut Cookies
Baklava Cigars
Greek Biscotta with Anise & Cinnamon
Honey Doughnuts
Sweet Custard Squares
Semi-Sweet Custard Purses
New Year's Day Cake
Cinnamon Biscuits
Warmed Figs with Walnuts
Watermelon & Feta Skewers
Greek Coffee

Braided Cookies

Koulouria (Koo-LOO-ree-ah)

These cookies can always be found in a Greek Grandma's cookie jar. They are a great dunking cookie. It takes a bit of practice to master the art of twisting the moist dough but once you get the hang of it it's pretty easy.

---

preparation 40 minutes   cooking 18-20 minutes   makes 65 cookies   bake 350°F (180°C)

---

6 ¼ cups cake & pastry flour
1 tbsp baking powder
½ tsp vanilla powder
½ cup milk
1 tsp ammonium bicarbonate
½ tsp baking soda
1 cup unsalted butter, melted
1½ cups sugar
3 eggs
Olive oil for greasing
1 egg yolk
1 tbsp milk
¼ cup sesame seeds

AMMONIUM BICARBONATE
Ammonium bicarbonate makes pastries very light and fluffy. If you cannot find ammonium bicarbonate then substitute it with baking powder in equal proportions.

MAKE AHEAD
Braided cookies can be stored in an airtight container for up to 2 weeks.

Sift 1 cup of the flour in a small bowl. Add the baking powder and vanilla powder and set aside.

Warm the milk in a small saucepan over low heat. Stir in the ammonium bicarbonate and baking soda. Remove from the heat and set aside.

Add the butter, sugar and eggs to the mixing bowl of a stand mixer fitted with a whisk attachment. Beat on medium speed until smooth. Add the warm milk mixture set aside earlier and continue beating. Reduce the speed to low and add the flour and powder mix set aside earlier. Continue beating until all of the ingredients are combined.

Using a rubber spatula, transfer the batter into a large bowl. Add the remaining flour one cup at a time and use your hand to blend. The dough will be moist and slightly sticky.

Lightly grease your hands and a flat work surface. Scoop a tablespoon of dough and roll it into a 6-inch (about 15cm) rope. Gather the ends of the rope together with one hand and use your other hand to twist the dough three times to create a braid or twisted effect. Place the braided cookie on a parchment paper-lined baking sheet. Repeat these steps with the remaining dough, spacing the cookies about 1-inch (2.5cm) apart.

Whisk the egg yolk and milk in a small bowl and brush over the cookies. Sprinkle with sesame seeds. Place the braided cookies in the middle of a preheated oven and bake for 18 minutes, or until lightly golden.

Almond Butter Cookies

Kourambiedes (Koo-rahm-bee-EH-des)

These "snow-covered" cookies make a beautiful display during the Christmas holidays. They are filled with almonds and have a hint of Ouzo. Confectioner's sugar is added once the cookies are baked and removed hot from the oven. They are dusted again once the cookies have cooled.

---

preparation 15 minutes   cooking 20 minutes   makes 65 cookies   bake 350°F (180°C)

---

4 ½ cups cake & pastry flour
1 tsp baking powder
1 tsp baking soda
2 egg yolks
1 egg, whole
2/3 cup sugar
1 tbsp Ouzo
2 cups unsalted butter, melted
¼ tsp vanilla extract
1 cup almonds, slivered
Confectioner's sugar for dusting

MAKE AHEAD .
Cookies can be stored in an airtight container for 3-4 weeks. Sprinkle with more Confectioner's sugar just before serving.

USE COOKIE CUTTERS
This is a great cookie cutter dough. We like to use holiday cutters for these cookies around Christmas time.

Sift 2 tablespoons of the flour with the baking powder and baking soda in a small bowl and set aside.

Add the eggs, sugar and Ouzo to the mixing bowl of a stand mixer fitted with a whisk attachment. Whisk for 3 minutes on medium speed. Add the butter and vanilla and whisk for a further 2 minutes.

Add the sifted ingredients set aside earlier and mix until combined. Stir in the almonds.

Change the mixer attachment to a dough hook and add the remaining flour 1 cup at a time. The dough should be moist and hold together well.

Begin shaping the cookies by taking 1 tablespoon of dough into your hands. Roll the dough into a ball and press your thumb gently in the center of the ball to make a small indentation. Place the cookie on a parchment paper-lined baking sheet. Repeat these steps with the remaining dough, spacing the cookies 1-inch (2.5cm) apart.

Place the baking sheet in the middle of a preheated oven for 20 minutes, or until the cookies are golden brown.

Leave the cookies on the baking sheet and generously dust them with Confectioner's sugar while they are still warm. Transfer to a cooling rack. Sprinkle the cooled cookies with more Confectioner's sugar and line them with a decorative cup. Transfer to a serving platter.

Honey-Dipped Walnut Cookies

Melomakarona (Meh-loh-mah-KAH-roh-nah)

These cookies are moist and delicious. Just a bit of oil and flour hold this cookie together. They are flavoured with cinnamon, cloves, orange zest and brandy. The baked cookies are drenched in honey and topped with walnuts. No Greek home is without them at Christmas time.

preparation 45 minutes	cooking 25 minutes	makes 60 cookies	bake 350°F (180°C)

FOR THE COOKIE DOUGH
½ cup sugar
½ tsp baking soda
2 tsp baking powder
½ tsp cinnamon, ground
½ tsp cloves, ground
2 cups corn oil
½ cup fresh orange juice
1 tsp orange zest
1 tsp lemon zest
1 tbsp Metaxa, or other brandy
5 cups cake & pastry flour, sifted, plus ¼ cup reserve

FOR THE HONEY SYRUP
2 cups honey
2 cups water
2 tbsp lemon juice
2 tsp lemon zest
4 cloves, whole
2 cinnamon sticks

1 cup walnut crumbs

MAKE AHEAD
Melomakarona that have not been dipped in the honey syrup can be stored in an airtight container for up to 2 months.

Add all of the cookie dough ingredients except the flour to the mixing bowl of a stand mixer fitted with a whisk attachment. Mix on low speed until combined.

Change the mixer attachment to a dough hook and add the flour one cup at a time. Mix on low speed. Scrape down the sides of the bowl with a rubber spatula if needed. The cookie dough will be oily.

Scoop about 1 tablespoon of dough into a ball and then shape it into an oval. Gently press the prongs of a fork partway through the oval cookie three times. These holes will help the honey syrup soak into the cookie later. Place on a parchment paper-lined baking sheet. Repeat these steps with the remaining dough, spacing the cookies 1-inch (2.5cm) apart.

Place the baking sheet in the middle of a preheated oven for 25 minutes, or until golden brown. Transfer the cookies to a cooling rack.

To prepare the honey syrup add the syrup ingredients to a small saucepan over high heat. Bring to a boil. Remove any white foam that forms at the surface of the syrup with a spoon.

Reduce the heat and immerse the baked cookies in the hot syrup for 2 minutes. Do not overcrowd the pan; work in batches.

Remove the honey dipped cookies with a slotted spoon and immediately sprinkle them with some walnut crumbs. Line the cookies with a decorative cup and transfer to a serving platter.

Baklava Cigars

Baklava se Pourro (Bah-klah-VAH seh POO-roh)

Mention Greek dessert and everyone thinks Baklava. It is found in every Greek restaurant and tavern. In this recipe, we have shown how Baklava can be rolled into cigars. It is a popular variation that is easier to serve and eat!

---

preparation 30 minutes   cooking 30 minutes   makes 20 pieces   bake 350°F (180°C)

FOR THE SYRUP
1 cup water
1½ cups sugar
½ cup honey
1 tsp fresh lemon juice
1 tsp lemon zest
1 cinnamon stick
2 cloves, whole
2 tbsp Metaxa or other
brandy (optional)

FOR THE BAKLAVA
2 cups walnuts or
almonds, finely chopped
¼ cup breadcrumbs
¼ cup sugar
2 tsp cinnamon, ground
½ tsp cloves, ground
½ cup unsalted butter
10 sheets phyllo pastry,
thawed

In a small saucepan bring the syrup ingredients (excluding the brandy) to a boil over high heat. Stir occasionally. Reduce the heat and let it simmer for 5 minutes. Using a spoon, remove any foam that forms at the surface. Add the Metaxa if desired. Set aside and let it cool completely.

For the baklava, mix the walnuts with the breadcrumbs, sugar, ground cinnamon and ground cloves in a bowl and set aside.

In a small saucepan, melt the butter over low heat. Remove from the heat and skim any foam. Use only the clarified butter and avoid the white milk solids that have settled at the bottom of the pan.

Lay 1 phyllo sheet in front of you horizontally and cover the remaining sheets with a damp cloth to avoid drying out. Use a pastry brush to lightly brush the phyllo with some melted butter. Grab the right end of the phyllo sheet and fold the phyllo in half like a book. Lightly brush with some more butter.

Spoon 3 tablespoons of the nut mixture along the narrow end of the phyllo leaving a ½-inch (12mm) border. Fold the sides over to enclose the filling and roll up. Lay the baklava cigar in a 9x13-inch (23x33cm) metal cake pan, seam-side down and brush the top with some butter.

Repeat this process with the remaining pieces of phyllo.

Using the tip of a sharp knife lightly score each roll in half without cutting all the way through to the filling.

Sprinkle some water on top of the baklava and place the pan in the middle of a preheated oven for 30 minutes or until golden-brown and crisp.

Remove the pan from the oven and immediately pour the cooled syrup on top of the hot baklava. The syrup should sizzle as it touches the phyllo pastry.

Let the baklava sit covered in plastic wrap at room temperature for several hours or overnight before serving so that the phyllo pastry has had time to absorb the syrup.

Cut along the scored lines again all the way through to the bottom of the pan and serve.

MAKE AHEAD
Baklava can be stored in an airtight container for 3 days. Baklava also freezes well before and after baking.

PHYLLO PASTRY TIPS

Always defrost phyllo pastry in the refrigerator overnight.

If you are pressed for time, you may defrost phyllo at room temperature for one hour; however, it may be more difficult to work with.

Any phyllo that you are not working with should be covered with a damp cloth to avoid drying out.

Rips or tears can easily be mended by brushing the sheet with butter and patching it up with another piece of phyllo.

Greek Biscotta with Anise & Cinnamon

Paximadia (Pah-ksee-MAH-dee-ah)

The baking process of Greek biscotta is very similar to Italian biscotti; the biscuits are baked two times to perfection, first in a log shape and then in slices. The combination of vanilla, anise, cinnamon and walnuts make these biscotta very aromatic and flavourful. Store bought versions don't even come close.

---

preparation 15 minutes   cooking 40 minutes   makes 24   bake 350°F (180°C)

2¼ cups all-purpose flour
¾ cup sugar
1½ tsp baking powder
1 tsp cinnamon, ground
½ tsp salt
½ cup vegetable oil
3 eggs, beaten
½ tsp vanilla extract
½ tsp anise seed
Flour for dusting
¾ cup walnuts, chopped
1 egg yolk, beaten
2 tsp sesame seeds

VARIATIONS
You can always add different fillings to your biscotta. Cranberries, almonds, pistachios or chopped dried figs are all wonderful ideas. Once you've mastered the technique give them a try!

STORING
Biscotta can be stored in an airtight container for up to two weeks.

Use a wooden spoon to combine the flour, sugar, baking powder, cinnamon and salt in a large mixing bowl. Make a well in the centre.

Add the oil, eggs, vanilla and anise seed. Use your hands to mix the wet and dry ingredients together. The dough that forms should be moist and light brown in colour.

Transfer the dough to a lightly dusted work surface. Divide into two equal pieces.

Use a rolling pin to flatten out one piece of dough until it is about ¼-inch (6mm) thick. Top the entire surface of the dough with half of the walnuts. Roll the dough back up and shape it into a log measuring 12-inches (30cm) long and ½-inch (12mm) thick. Repeat with the other piece of dough.

Place the two logs on a rimless baking sheet lined with parchment paper. Use a pastry brush to lightly brush the top of the dough with the beaten egg yolk. Sprinkle the logs with sesame seeds.

Bake in a preheated oven for 30 minutes until lightly golden. Transfer the logs to a cooling rack. Cool for 5 minutes. Transfer to a cutting board and use a serrated knife to slice the logs into 1-inch (2.5cm) thick slices. Lay the cookies flat on the baking sheet and bake for another 10 minutes.

Remove from the oven and serve.

Honey Doughnuts

Loukoumades (Loo-koo-MAH-dehs)

These small doughnut bites are covered with honey and dusted with cinnamon. They are melt-in-your-mouth delicious.

---

preparation 1 hour 30 minutes   cooking 25 minutes   makes 50-60 doughnuts

---

1½ tsp active dry yeast
2 cups warm water
2½ cups all-purpose flour
1 egg
¼ cup milk
Vegetable oil for frying
Honey
Cinnamon, ground
Confectioner's sugar

THERMOMETER
If using an oil thermometer, heat the oil until it reaches 350°F (180°C).

Mix the yeast with ¼ cup of the warm water and 2 tablespoons of the flour in a large mixing bowl. Set aside for 5 minutes.

Add the egg, milk, remaining flour and warm water to the large mixing bowl. Mix with a wooden spoon until combined. Set the mixture aside in a warm place for 1 hour until the batter expands to almost double its size with pockets of air bubbles.

Carefully move the mixing bowl next to the stove top. Do not agitate the bubbles that have formed in the dough.

Fill a sauté pan that is no more than 3-inches (7.5cm) deep half way with oil. Heat the oil over high heat and test the oil by dropping ¼ teaspoon of dough into the oil. Once the dough turns brown, the oil is hot enough to use. If the oil smokes, turn the heat down.

Working in batches, use a teaspoon to drop spoonfuls of batter into the hot oil. Each teaspoon of batter should sizzle and expand into a fluffy round doughnut. Rest the spoon in a warm cup of water in between batches. Dry off the spoon before placing it in the batter again.

Turn the doughnuts with tongs and remove them with a slotted spoon when lightly golden brown on all sides. Place the doughnuts on a plate lined with paper towel to absorb the excess oil.

Transfer the prepared doughnuts to a serving platter and generously coat with honey. Sprinkle with cinnamon and Confectioner's sugar. Serve warm.

Sweet Custard Squares

Yalaktoboureko (Yah-lah-ktoh-BOO-ree-koh)

Yalaktoboureko is a light milk custard topped with a flaky pastry that is soaked in syrup. This dessert is delicious and easy to prepare. It's a Greek classic, right up there with Baklava.

---

preparation 20 minutes   cooking 45 minutes   makes 12 pieces   bake 350°F (180°C)

FOR THE MILK CUSTARD
4 cups milk
¾ cup semolina
1 cup sugar
4 eggs, lightly beaten
½ tsp vanilla extract
Zest of ½ lemon

FOR THE SYRUP
1 cup sugar
2 cups water
1 tsp lemon juice
1 cinnamon stick
Zest of ½ lemon

½ cup unsalted butter, melted
10 sheets phyllo pastry, thawed

MAKE AHEAD
Sweet phyllo and milk custard squares can be stored in the refrigerator for 2 days and can be served cold.

See phyllo pastry tips on page 221.

To prepare the milk custard add the milk to a large pot over medium heat. When the milk is warm, slowly whisk in the semolina. Add the sugar, eggs, vanilla and lemon zest and whisk constantly until the milk thickens. The custard will have a porridge-like consistency. Remove from the heat and set aside.

Using a wooden spoon, mix all of the syrup ingredients in a small saucepan over high heat. Bring to a boil and reduce the heat to medium. Maintain a low boil for 5 minutes. Set the syrup aside and remove the cinnamon stick. Let it cool completely.

Melt the butter in a small saucepan over low heat. Remove from the heat and skim away any foam. Use only the clarified butter and avoid the white milk solids that have settled at the bottom of the pan.

Use a pastry brush to grease a 9x12-inch (23x23cm) metal cake pan with some of the melted butter.

Gather two of the phyllo sheets and cover the remaining sheets with a damp cloth to avoid drying out. Lay the two sheets of phyllo along the bottom of the pan. Allow the two sheets to overlap at the center of the pan and the excess phyllo to hang over the sides of the pan. Brush these sheets lightly with some melted butter.

Arrange another two sheets of phyllo in the same manner, this time allowing the excess phyllo to hang over the opposite sides of the pan. Brush the sheets lightly with some melted butter. The baking pan should now have phyllo sheets hanging over every side of the pan.

Repeat this process using another four layers of phyllo pastry, brushing each sheet with some melted butter.

Pour the custard into the pan and smooth the surface using a rubber spatula.

Gather the excess phyllo pastry hanging over the sides of the pan and fold over the custard. This will encase the custard and protect it while baking. Brush each sheet with some melted butter.

Lay the remaining sheets of phyllo on the custard. Brush each sheet with some melted butter. Tuck the sheets of phyllo into the sides of the pan. Anything that cannot be tucked in neatly should be cut away with scissors.

Using a sharp knife, score the top layers of phyllo into squares.

Sprinkle some water on the custard squares and place the pan in the middle of a preheated oven for 45 minutes until golden brown.

Remove from the oven and immediately pour the cooled syrup on the hot custard squares.

Cool at room temperature for 1 hour before cutting along the scored lines to the bottom of the pan.

Serve warm or cold.

Semi-Sweet Custard Purses

Bougatsa (Boo-GAH-tsah)

This is a light dessert that always seems to get the most ooohs and aaahs. It is not syrupy like most popular Greek desserts. It is light, flaky and just perfect.

---

preparation 45 minutes   cooking 20 minutes   makes 18 purses   bake 350°F (180°C)

¾ cup semolina
¾ cup sugar
2 eggs
3 cups milk
Zest of ½ lemon
1/3 cup unsalted butter
10 sheets phyllo pastry, thawed
Confectioner's sugar
Cinnamon, ground

MAKE AHEAD
The custard can be made and refrigerated up to 1 day in advance of serving day. Completed custard purses can also be wrapped in waxed paper and frozen for up to 1 month. Thaw completely before baking.

See phyllo pastry tips on page 221.

Add the semolina, sugar and eggs to the mixing bowl of a stand mixer fitted with a whisk attachment. Mix on medium speed until the mixture is creamy, smooth and light yellow in colour, about 2 minutes.

Pour the batter into a large pot. Place the pot on the stove-top and slowly whisk in the milk. Increase the heat to medium-high. Whisk often so that the batter dissolves into the milk and does not stick to the bottom of the pot.

The batter will foam and thicken before it reaches its boiling point. This may take up to 10 minutes. Remove the custard from the heat once the custard is thick and the first few bubbles have formed.

Stir in the grated lemon zest and set aside to cool slightly.

Melt the butter in a small saucepan over low heat. Remove from the heat and skim away any foam. Use only the clarified butter and avoid the white milk solids that have settled at the bottom of the pan.

Roll out the phyllo pastry sheets. Use a sharp knife or kitchen scissors to cut the sheets into 4 square pieces of equal size. You should now have 40 sheets of phyllo. Take two squares of phyllo and cover the remaining squares with a damp cloth to avoid drying out. Use a pastry brush to coat the two phyllo squares with some melted butter. Stack the two squares of phyllo.

Place two tablespoons of the cooled custard filling in the centre of the phyllo square. Gather the phyllo at the corners and pinch the phyllo together at the centre to create a small purse with a ruffled top.

Rest the custard purse in a muffin tray to help maintain its shape while preparing the remaining purses. Repeat with the remaining pieces of phyllo.

Transfer the prepared custard purses to a parchment paper-lined baking sheet. Lightly brush with the remaining melted butter and place in a preheated oven for 20 minutes until golden-brown and flaky.

Transfer to a cooling rack with a spatula. Cool for 10 minutes.

Generously sprinkle the tops of each custard purse with Confectioner's sugar and cinnamon before serving.

Serve warm or at room temperature.

New Year's Day Cake

Vassilopita (Vah-see-LOH-pee-tah)

A traditional cake that we all look forward to eating after New Year's Day dinner. Not only is it delicious and light, but it has a lucky coin hiding inside it. The eldest member in the house takes it upon themselves to cut the cake, and pass a piece to every family member. The one that finds the hidden coin in their piece of cake is said to have good luck for the year.

preparation 25 minutes   cooking 60 minutes   bake 300°F (150°C)

3 cups cake & pastry flour
3 tsp baking powder
6 large eggs, separated, room temperature
¾ cup unsalted butter
¾ cup fresh orange juice
1 cup sugar
1 tsp orange zest
2 tsp Metaxa, or other brandy (optional)
Butter for greasing
Honey for spreading
Confectioner's sugar

Sift the flour and baking powder in a small bowl and set aside.

Add the egg whites to the mixing bowl of a stand mixer fitted with a whisk attachment, and mix on high speed until stiff white peaks form. Gently transfer to another bowl and set aside.

Melt the butter in a small saucepan over low heat. Remove from the heat and skim away the foam. Pour the clarified butter into a bowl and discard the white milk solids that have settled at the bottom of the pan. Stir in the orange juice and set aside.

Cream the egg yolks by adding the yolks and sugar to the mixing bowl of the stand mixer and whisk on medium-high speed until the mixture becomes a pale light yellow colour. On low speed pour in the butter and orange juice set aside earlier. Whisk until combined. Stir in the orange zest and brandy.

Gather the ingredients that were set aside earlier and add half of the sifted flour mixture and half of the whipped egg whites to the batter. Mix on low speed until combined. Add the remaining flour and egg whites to the batter and mix until smooth.

Pour the batter into a greased 9-inch (23cm) round springform pan and place in the middle of a preheated oven. Bake until the cake is golden and pulls away from the pan, about 60 minutes. Allow the cake to cool and then remove from the cake pan. Spread a thin layer of honey on the cake and dust with Confectioner's sugar. Serve.

HIDING THE COIN
If you plan to hide a coin in the cake, then be sure to wash the coin and wrap it in aluminum foil. Drop the coin into the batter right before pouring the batter into the cake pan.

Cinnamon Biscuits

Moskokoulouria (Moh-skoh-koo-LOO-ree-ah)

We love these cookies! The combination of cinnamon, cloves and orange gives these cookies a unique spiciness. They are perfect with coffee. We confess that the dough is a bit tricky to handle. The twisted shape on the right looks fabulous, but it takes some practice. The simple shapes below were made with cookie cutters, they are perfectly acceptable and taste just as good!

preparation 10 minutes	cooking 15 minutes	makes 50-60 cookies	bake 350°F (180°C)

2 cups vegetable oil
1 cup sugar
1 cup fresh orange juice
1 tsp baking soda
4 tsp baking powder
1 tsp orange zest
2 tsp cinnamon, ground
2 tsp clove, ground
6¼ cups cake & pastry flour

MAKE AHEAD
Cinnamon Biscuits can be stored in an airtight container for up to 2 weeks.

TIP
If using cookie cutters, flatten the dough to a ¼-inch (6mm) thickness directly on the parchment paper. This will save you the step of transferring the dough.

Add the oil and sugar to a large mixing bowl and whisk until combined.

In a small bowl, add the orange juice and baking soda and mix. Pour into the large mixing bowl and whisk until combined. Whisk in the remaining ingredients. Add the flour one cup at a time and mix by hand until you have a soft, oily and workable dough .

Use about 1 tablespoon of the dough to create an assortment of shapes by hand. Use cookie cutters if desired, see tip.

Place the cookies on a parchment paper-lined baking sheet, spaced 1-inch (2.5cm) apart. Bake in the middle of a preheated oven for 15 minutes or until brown. Transfer to a cooling rack. Serve .

Warmed Figs with Walnuts

Sika me Karidia (SEE-kah meh Kah-REE-dee-ah)

This is the perfect after-dinner treat alongside a tray of cheeses and a sweet digestif.

---

preparation 5 minutes   cooking 5 minutes   makes 4   bake 300°F (150°C)

---

4 dried figs
4 walnut halves

Open the dried fig in half with your fingers. Gently press the figs closed again and place on a baking sheet.

Place in the middle of a preheated oven for 5 minutes.

Transfer the figs to a serving dish and stuff the inside with a walnut halve.

Serve.

Watermelon & Feta Skewers

Karpouzi me Feta (Kahr-POO-zee meh FEH-tah)

Our mother can't wait to bring fruit to the dinner table after supper. She will often bring out fruit before the dinner table has even been cleared. One day she scooped up some remnants of feta cheese and paired it with a slice of watermelon—the result, a tasty and unique dessert. We witnessed her invent this but as with many brilliant ideas, someone else came up with it too because it is now a much enjoyed treat throughout Greece. Sorry mom.

---

preparation 10 minutes

Watermelon
Feta cheese

Cut the watermelon in half and use a melon ball scoop to make watermelon balls.

Cut the feta cheese into 1-inch (2.5cm) cubes.

Thread one watermelon ball and one feta cube on a toothpick or party pick and arrange on a serving platter. Repeat these steps to create as many skewers as desired. Serve.

Greek Coffee

Ellinikos Cafes (Eh-lee-nee-KOS Kah-FEHS)

We started drinking Greek coffee at a very young age because it went hand-in-hand with good conversation. We would often turn our cups over after sipping and attempt to read our future from the coffee grinds. Our aunt would always indulge us by reading the grinds and telling us that we would all marry handsome young men one day—and sure enough we all did!
The reading of the Greek coffee cup is an age-old tradition that keeps both the young and the old entertained.

preparation 2 minutes   cooking 5 minutes   makes 2 coffees

METRIOS (REGULAR)
2 heaping tsp Greek coffee
2 tsp sugar
2 demitasse cups water

YLIKOS (SWEET)
2 heaping tsp Greek coffee
4 tsp sugar
2 demitasse cups water

SKETOS (BITTER)
2 heaping tsp Greek coffee
2 demitasse cups water

Decide on the strength of the coffee. The most common preference is a *metrios* (regular) coffee.

Place the coffee and sugar in the *briki* (see *Glossary, page 268)* and then add the water. Stir until combined.

Place the briki over high heat. Before the coffee boils it will form a layer of froth at the top. Slight bubbles will also form around the edges. When the coffee begins to rise and the froth boils over onto itself, immediately remove the briki from the heat. Do not let the coffee boil over longer, as this spoils the froth.

Pour 1/3 of the coffee into each cup. This ensures that the froth is shared between both cups. Pour the remaining coffee into each cup.

Serve alongside a tall glass of cold water and a sweet dessert.

HOW TO DRINK THE COFFEE

Allow the coffee to settle for a couple of minutes before drinking. Greek coffee is meant to be sipped slowly in between conversation. Unlike other coffees, the grinds of a Greek coffee are in the cup and they slowly settle to the bottom. Do not drink the last little sip of coffee–the coffee grinds are bitter!

Our aunts baked regularly and always dropped off a loaf or two of fresh bread to our parents' home. The loaves were often still warm and wrapped in tea towels. As children, there was nothing else quite as comforting or as delicious.

Breads

Basic Dough

Home-made Pitas with Feta Cheese

Sesame Rings

Sweet Easter Bread

Garlic Bread with Olive Oil

Basic Dough

Zimari (Zee-MAH-ree)

Bread—what would we do without it?
Use this dough recipe to make a loaf of bread, pizza, or *Home-made Pitas with Feta Cheese*.

---

preparation 1 hour 20 minutes

---

1 package active dry
yeast, (2 ½ tsp)
½ tsp salt
4 cups all-purpose flour,
plus 1 cup reserve
2 cups warm water
Olive oil for coating

MIXERS
Use your hands if you
don't have a mixer.
Add the flour 1 cup at a
time.

In a small bowl, add the yeast, salt and 2 tablespoons of the flour. Pour in ½ cup of the warm water and mix with a wooden spoon until combined. Let it rest for 10 minutes.

Transfer the mixture to the mixing bowl of a stand mixer fitted with a dough hook.

Add the remaining flour and water to the mixing bowl and mix on low speed until it is a workable dough. Add up to 1 cup reserved flour if needed.

Lightly coat the dough with olive oil. Cover the mixing bowl with a cloth and set aside in a warm, draft-free area for at least an hour until the dough has doubled in size.

The dough is ready for use.

Home-made Pitas with Feta Cheese

Tiyanites Pites (Tee-yah-nee-TEHS PEE-tehs)

Whenever our mom made pizza, she would always set aside some dough and make home-made pitas for breakfast or lunch the next day. These pitas were topped with heaps of feta cheese—we could never get enough of them! If there are little ones in your life include them in this prep. They will love handling the dough and knowing they helped make their own meal.

preparation 10 minutes   cooking 20 minutes   makes 10

Basic Dough recipe, see page 244

Olive oil for greasing
2 tbsp olive oil per pita
Feta cheese, crumbled, as desired

Divide the dough into 10 equal pieces. Roll each piece into a ball.

Lightly oil a work surface. Take one ball of dough and use a rolling pin to flatten it into a 6-inch (15cm) round pita. (It does not have to be perfectly round.)

Heat about 2 tablespoons of olive oil in a frying pan over medium-high heat. Lay the pita in the frying pan and reduce the heat to medium-low. Fry until lightly golden-brown on both sides, about 2 minutes per side. The pita will bubble as it cooks.

Remove the pita from the pan and place on a platter lined with paper towel to absorb any excess oil.

Repeat this process with the remaining balls of dough.

Crumble feta cheese down the middle of the pita, fold and serve.

Sesame Rings

Koulouria me Sousami (Koo-LOO-ree-ah meh Soo-SAH-mee)

Sesame rings are sold all over Greece by outdoor vendors. Their smell fills the streets and overwhelms children and adults alike. When shopping in Athens, we always succumbed to their taunting and never regretted it. Simply delicious.

preparation night before + 1 hour 15 minutes   cooking 15 minutes   makes 6   bake 430°F (225°C)

1 package active dry yeast, (2 ½ tsp)
1 cup warm water
2 tbsp all-purpose flour
2 cups all-purpose flour, plus 1 cup reserve
1 tsp salt
¼ cup sugar
2 tbsp olive oil
1 cup sesame seeds

The night before serving day, place ½ of the active dry yeast package (1¼ teaspoon) into a small bowl with ½ cup warm water and 1 tablespoon flour. Mix with a wooden spoon and let the mixture stand, covered in plastic wrap, overnight at room temperature. The next day the mixture will be bubbly, and have a slightly fermented smell.

To make the dough, place the remaining 1¼ teaspoon yeast, ½ cup warm water, and 1 tablespoon flour into a separate bowl. Mix with a wooden spoon and let it stand for 15 minutes.

Meanwhile, sift the 2 cups flour, salt and sugar into the mixing bowl of a stand mixer fitted with a dough hook. Make a well in the centre and add the oil and the two yeast containers prepared earlier. Mix on low speed until a dough forms. If the dough is runny, add up to 1 cup more flour. Alternatively, you can use your hands to knead the dough.

Cover the dough with a cloth and set aside in a warm, draft-free spot until the dough has doubled in size, about 1 hour.

Remove the dough from the bowl and punch down the dough with your hands for 2 minutes to remove the air bubbles. Divide the dough into 6 equal pieces using a sharp knife.

Roll out each of the 6 pieces of dough into a rope, about 16-inches (40cm) long. Immerse each rope into a cold water bath. Gently remove the ropes from the water bath and coat them entirely with sesame seeds.

Firmly press the ends of the ropes together to form a large ring. The hole in the centre of the ring is much larger than a traditional bagel ring. Arrange the 6 sesame rings on a parchment paper-lined baking sheet and place in the middle of a preheated oven for 15 minutes, or until they are a light brown colour.

Remove from the oven and transfer to a cooling rack. Enjoy warm or cold with your favourite spread or simply on their own.

Sweet Easter Bread

Tsoureki (Tsoo-REH-kee)

These braided breads line the windows of every Greek specialty shop during Easter. They are often adorned with colourful Easter eggs and are regarded as a symbol of blessing and fertility. Our mom would take great pride in baking them, and we took great pleasure in eating them.

---

preparation 30 minutes   cooking 40 minutes   makes 5 loaves   bake 320°F (160°C)

---

2 packages active dry
yeast, (5 tsp)
¼ cup warm water
1 tsp sugar
½ cup unsalted butter,
melted
½ cup vegetable oil
1½ cups sugar
6 eggs, room
temperature
1 cup milk, room
temperature
½ cup fresh squeezed
orange juice
1 tbsp orange zest
1 tsp Mahlepi, ground
1 tsp Mastiha, ground
8 cups all purpose flour,
plus ½ cup reserve
2 eggs
1 tbsp milk
½ cup sesame seeds

Gently stir the yeast, water and sugar together in a glass bowl and set aside for 10 minutes.

Transfer the yeast mixture to a large mixing bowl. Add the remaining ingredients up until the flour and whisk together until completely combined.

Add the flour to the mixing bowl one cup at a time and use your hand to mix. Once all of the flour has been added, knead the dough for 5-7 minutes.

Cover the dough with a clean kitchen towel and several blankets. Place in a warm, draft-free spot until the dough has doubled in size, about 1½ hours.

Transfer the risen dough to a clean work surface and punch it down. Cut the dough into 5 equal portions. Take one portion and set the remaining pieces aside.

Cut the portion into 3 equal pieces. Using your palms, and starting in the center, work to elongate the pieces of dough until they are about 12-inches (30cm) in length. The dough will want to pull together, you will need to pull on it to keep its length.

Line the 3 pieces of dough vertically on the work surface in front of you. Cross the right strand over the middle strand, then cross the left strand over the middle strand and keep repeating this braiding pattern until you reach the end of the dough.

Pinch the ends together at the top and bottom and tuck them under.

Place the braided loaf on a parchment-paper lined baking sheet, cover with a dry kitchen towel. Repeat with the other portions of dough. Let the braided dough rise again in a warm, draft-free spot until it doubles in size. This will take about an hour.

Whisk the egg and milk together in a small bowl. Brush the loaves with the egg wash and sprinkle with some sesame seeds. Place the loaves in a preheated oven and bake for 40 minutes or until golden brown. Transfer to a cooling rack and let cool completely before serving.

Garlic Bread with Olive Oil

Psomi me Skordo ke Ladi (Psoh-MEE meh SKOR-doh keh LAH-dee)

Our dad's famous garlic bread—well it is famous in our family. He likes to make it with olive oil and lots of garlic. In this recipe, we have suggested the use of two cloves of garlic, but this can easily be changed to suit your taste.

---

preparation 5 minutes   cooking 4 minutes   serves 6   broil 500°F (260°C)

1/3 cup olive oil
2 garlic cloves, pressed
1 baguette, sliced
lengthways

Combine the olive oil and garlic in a small bowl. Use a brush to coat each slice of the baguette with olive oil and garlic.

Place the bread in the upper-third of a preheated oven, directly on the oven rack. Broil for about 4 minutes, until the bread turns golden-brown.

Cut into pieces and serve.

The following sauces and dressings are as essential to the Greek kitchen as pots and pans.

No Greek kitchen is without them.

Sauces & Dressings

Basic Crushed Tomato Sauce for the Pantry
Fresh Tomato Sauce
Meat Sauce
Béchamel Sauce
Lemon & Egg Sauce
Tomato & Onion Relish
Lemon, Oregano & Olive Oil Dressing

Basic Crushed Tomato Sauce for the Pantry

Domata Salsa Sketi (Doh-MAH-tah SAHL-sah SKEH-tee)

A must in everyone's pantry. In the fall, we spend an entire day washing tomatoes, boiling tomatoes, and jarring tomatoes. We make hundreds of jars to divide amongst ourselves and to use throughout the year. It takes a lot of organization and cooperation. Although it's an exhausting day, it is well worth it. The following recipe gives you just a little glimpse as to what is involved and makes about two cups of sauce.

preparation 5 minutes   cooking 30 minutes   makes 2 cups

8 plum tomatoes, whole
½ tsp salt
¼ tsp pepper

MAKE AHEAD
A basic crushed tomato sauce can be kept in an airtight container in the refrigerator for 3 days.

Use a knife to mark the bottom of each plum tomato with an 'X'.

Plunge the marked tomatoes into a pot of boiling water.

After 5 minutes, remove the tomatoes with a slotted spoon.

When they are cool enough to handle, peel the skins of the tomatoes.

Cut the tomatoes in half and carefully remove the seeds with your fingers. Place them in a food processor and purée.

Add the puréed tomatoes to a saucepan over high heat and bring to a boil. Boil for 5 minutes. Reduce the heat and simmer until the sauce has thickened, about 15 minutes. Season with salt and pepper.

Allow to cool and transfer to a glass jar with a fitted lid.

Fresh Tomato Sauce

Domata Salsa Freski (Doh-MAH-tah SAHL-sah FREHS-Kee)

This recipe takes the basic tomato sauce recipe on the previous page and turns it into something just a little more complex. Perfect for topping your favourite pasta.

---

preparation 5 minutes   cooking 30 minutes   makes 2 cups

---

1 tbsp olive oil
2 garlic cloves, minced
2 cups crushed tomato sauce
1 tbsp oregano, dried
1 red chili pepper, dried (optional)
Salt & pepper to taste
1 basil sprig, chopped

Heat the olive oil in a saucepan over medium heat. Add the garlic and sauté for 1 minute.

Add the crushed tomato sauce and bring the ingredients to a boil.

Add the oregano, and chili pepper if desired. Season with salt and pepper to taste.

Lower the heat and simmer until the sauce has thickened, about 20 minutes. Toss in the basil and serve.

Meat Sauce

Salsa me Kreas (SAHL-sah meh KREH-ahs)

Use this meat sauce for the following recipes in this cookbook: *Moussaka, Baked Penne topped with Béchamel Sauce* and *Eggplant Slippers*.

---

preparation 10 minutes   cooking 45 minutes   makes 2 cups

1lb (500g) ground beef, extra lean
1½ tsp salt
1 yellow onion, chopped
1 cup red wine
1 tbsp tomato paste
2 cups crushed tomato sauce
1 tbsp oregano, dried
Pepper to taste
¼ cup fresh basil and parsley, chopped

MAKE AHEAD
Meat Sauce can be stored in the freezer for up to 3 months.

Brown the ground beef in a large sauté pan over medium-high heat. Add salt to the ground beef as it cooks. Break up the ground beef using a wooden spoon. Drain the fat if needed.

Lower the heat to medium and add the onion. Sauté until the onions are soft, about 5 minutes.

Add the wine and cook until the wine is reduced by half.

Add the tomato paste, crushed tomato sauce, oregano and pepper. Bring sauce to a boil, lower the heat and simmer until the sauce has thickened, about 30 minutes. If the sauce is too thick, add some water.

Stir in the chopped fresh herbs and remove from the heat.

Béchamel Sauce

Krema Beshamel (KREH-mah Beh-shah-MEL)

This creamy sauce tops the following recipes: *Moussaka* and *Baked Penne topped with Béchamel Sauce*. It can also top the *Eggplant Slippers* recipe.

---

preparation 5 minutes   cooking 15 minutes   makes about 4 cups

---

½ cup butter
½ cup all-purpose flour
4 cups milk, homo,
warmed
2 tbsp Mizithra cheese or
Pecorino Romano,
grated
¼ tsp salt
¼ tsp nutmeg

MAKE AHEAD
Béchamel Sauce can
be made up to 2 days in
advance and
refrigerated until ready
for use.

Melt the butter in a saucepan over medium heat. Add the flour and mix with a wooden spatula until the flour and butter are combined.

Gradually add the milk and whisk continuously to avoid any lumps from forming. Simmer until the sauce is thick and creamy, about 10 minutes. Remove the sauce from the heat just before it reaches its boiling point.

Add the cheese, salt and nutmeg. Set aside until ready for use.

Lemon & Egg Sauce

Avgolemmono (Ahv-goh-LEH-moh-noh)

This sauce gives meals a creamy consistency and is prepared just before serving the dish to guests. It is unique to the Greek kitchen. It is used in the following recipes in this cookbook: *Artichokes & Potatoes with Dill, Chicken Soup, Meatball Soup, Pork & Celery Stew.*

---

preparation 5 minutes

---

2 eggs, separated
¼ cup fresh lemon juice
1 cup broth, from the dish
that you are making the
sauce for

In a medium bowl, whisk the egg whites on high speed using a hand mixer. Whisk until thickened white and foamy.

While whisking, slowly add the egg yolks followed by the lemon juice.

Gradually add the hot broth. This is known as tempering the eggs.

Add this *Lemon and Egg sauce* to your soup or stew dish. Allow the sauce to heat through but do not let it boil as this will make the eggs curdle.

This sauce will thicken your soup or stew and will also give it a creamy consistency.

Tomato & Onion Relish

Salsa Domatas ke Kremidi (SAHL-sah Doh-MAH-tahs keh Kreh-MEE-dee)

This savoury relish is best enjoyed on top of baked or fried cod, see *Baked Cod with a Tomato & Onion Relish*. It is also a wonderful topping for *Fried Potatoes*.

---

preparation 5 minutes   cooking 35 minutes   makes 1 cup

1/3 cup olive oil
2 yellow onions, sliced
1 tomato, chopped
3 garlic cloves, sliced
1 tbsp tomato paste
½ cup water
1 tsp rosemary, dried
½ tsp salt & pepper

MAKE AHEAD
The relish can be made and refrigerated up to one day in advance of serving day until ready for use. Reheat on the stove-top just before serving.

Heat the olive oil in a large sauté pan over medium heat.

Lower the heat and add the onion. Sauté until soft and caramelized, about 15 minutes.

Add the chopped tomato and garlic to the pan. Sauté for 2 to 3 minutes.

In a small bowl, mix the tomato paste with ½ cup water. Add it to the sauté pan and bring the sauce to a boil. Reduce the heat and season with rosemary, salt and pepper. Simmer for 15 minutes or until all of the liquid has been absorbed and the sauce is thick.

Serve.

Lemon, Oregano & Olive Oil Dressing

Ladoriyani (Lah-doh-REE-yah-nee)

The quintessential dressing of the Greek kitchen. It can be added to any grilled meat or fish.

preparation 5 minutes   makes about ½ cup

1/3 cup olive oil
¼ cup fresh lemon juice
½ tsp oregano, dried
½ tsp salt

Whisk the ingredients in a small mixing bowl. Set aside until ready for use.

Seasonal Menu Ideas

Spring

Saganaki

Tomato Fennel Soup

Beef Tenderloin Stuffed with Figs
& Apricots
Red Roasted Potatoes

Semi-Sweet Custard Purses

Summer

Santorini Croquettes

Tomato & Cucumber Village
Salad

Grilled Whole Red Snapper
Cinnamon & Clove Potatoes

Honey Doughnuts

Fall

Baked Pumpkin Fritters

Baked Cod with a Tomato &
Onion Relish
Garlic & Olive Oil Mashed
Potatoes
Garlic Beet Salad

Sweet Custard Squares

Winter

Olive Tapenade & Goat Cheese
on Pita Chips

Lentil Soup

Braised Rabbit with Pearl Onions
Fried Potatoes

Honey-Dipped Walnut Cookies

Special Occasion Menu Ideas

Easter

Feta-Stuffed Phyllo Pastry Bites

Zucchini Ribbon Rolls

Roasted Leg of Lamb
Artichokes & Potatoes with Dill

Sweet Easter Bread

Backyard Barbecue

Grilled Octopus
Spirit of Ouzo

Santorini-Style Souvlaki on a Pita
Grilled Summer Vegetables

Watermelon & Feta Skewers

Kid-Friendly

Parsley & Mint Meatballs

Zucchini Chips

Baked Penne Topped with
Béchamel Sauce

Braided Cookies

Picnic

Fish Roe Dip

Stuffed Grape Leaves

Zucchini Tart
Potato & White Bean Salad

Cinnamon Biscuits

Casual Vegetarian

Zucchini Chips

Chickpea Burgers
Roasted Pepper Salad

Greek Biscotta with Anise &
Cinnamon

Formal Vegetarian

Spanakopita

Salmon with Sun-Dried Tomatoes
Paprika Potatoes
Lemon Asparagus

Baklava Cigars

Christmas

Fried Calamari
Marinated Olives

Pork Medallions Stuffed with
Sun-Dried Tomatoes & Goat
Cheese
Roasted Vegetables

Almond Butter Cookies

New Year's Eve

Shrimp with Ouzo & Red Chilies

Stuffed Sweet Peppers

Fresh Herb-Crusted Rack of Lamb
Lemon Potatoes

New Year's Day Cake

Glossary

Ammonium Bicarbonate A white powder that is used in baking. It gives baked goods a lighter and crispier texture than baking soda or baking powder. Ammonium bicarbonate should be stored in an airtight container in a cool, dry place. Stored properly, ammonium bicarbonate can last for several years. To test whether your ammonium bicarbonate is still active, drop a teaspoon of powder into a cup with vinegar or lemon juice – active ammonium bicarbonate will fizz when it comes into contact with these acidic juices.

Anise Seed A gray-brown oval seed used to flavour baked goods, sweets and liquors. It smells and tastes like black licorice.

Béchamel A basic white sauce made with milk and roux (butter and flour). This sauce tops traditional dishes like Moussaka and Pastitsio.

Briki This is a traditional pot used for boiling Greek coffee. It is made of copper and lined with tin. Most briki sizes allow you to make 2, 4 or 6 demitasse cups of coffee. Nowadays, most people use stainless steel coffee pots – these are the same pots that are used to froth milk for cappuccino or café lattes.

Dandelions The most nutritionally dense greens you can eat! It is an underappreciated "weed" in North America. In Greece, dandelions replace the lettuce salad at the dinner table. They are most often served with olive oil, lemon and a pinch of salt.

Elephant Beans The Greek Elephant bean is a giant white kidney bean that is highly nutritious. They originate in Northern Greece and are known for their giant size, kidney shape, and snow-white colour. Lima beans can be substituted but they do not have the characteristic kidney shape and they are not as flavourful.

Feta Cheese A soft or lightly crumbly white sheep's milk cheese. You can find this cheese in just about every supermarket but finding real Greek feta is a little more challenging. Greek food stores and markets with a wide range of international cheese selections will sell you *real* Greek feta and you will immediately notice a sharper, saltier and richer flavour!

Greek Coffee The beans of a Greek coffee are ground until they are a fine powder. Greek coffee is made in a traditional Greek coffee pot called a *briki*.

Greek Extra Virgin Olive Oil A 100% natural cold pressed olive oil. The olive oil comes from the first pressing of the olives without any chemicals or hot water added. Make sure to check the label on the oil containers to ensure that the oil is a product of Greece.

Greek Sausage The distinguishing flavour of a Greek sausage is the orange rind and wine that it contains. Greek sausage is sold uncooked and tastes best when fried or barbecued.

Kefalotiri Cheese A tangy, salty hard cheese made from sheep's or goat's milk. It is left to age for three to four months before being sent to markets. It is a great cheese to serve as an appetizer alongside marinated olives. This cheese is also needed to make the famous saganaki that you see in most Greek restaurants. Kefalotiri can be found in markets that carry a wide range of international cheese selections. A good substitute for kefalotiri is parmesan or asiago cheese.

Kritharaki A pasta that looks and cooks like rice. It is commonly known as orzo. The amount of water needed to make kritharaki is crucial to its success. Using a 1:3 ratio of kritharaki to water is appropriate.

Mahlepi Greek mahlepi spice is a finely-ground off-white powder. It is an unusual spice with a fruity taste. It is made from the inner kernels of the fruit pits from Persian cherry trees. It is this unusual spice that distinguishes Greek Easter bread from any other bread.

Mastiha Originally used as a chewing gum, mastiha is the sap found in evergreen bushes. It comes in the form of resinous granules, but can sometimes be found in powdered form. It is used in sweets.

Mavrodaphne A very sweet red dessert wine. Originating in Peloponnese Greece, this wine has a nice fruity flavour. It can be found at your local liquor store. Mavrodaphne substitutions: Madeira, Banyuls, or other sweet red dessert wines.

Metaxa Brandy A Greek distilled spirit, it is essentially a blend of brandy and wine. It comes in 5 varieties, Three Stars, Five Stars, Seven Stars, Twelve Stars, and the Grand Reserve.

Mezes Small portions or starters. A typical meze platter would consist of octopus, dolmades, olives, calamari, and various salty cheeses. Ouzo would be the spirit of choice to accompany such foods. Equivalent to Spanish tapas.

Mizithra Cheese A soft sheep or goat milk cheese made from leftover whey. Aged Mizithra comes in the shape of a large hard ball. Finely grate part of it and keep it handy in your fridge. Place the rest of the Mizithra in your freezer for a later date. You can find this cheese in specialty cheese shops and you can even have it delivered to your home. An acceptable substitute for Mizithra is romano cheese; however, it is important to note that the authentic flavour of the recipes in this cookbook will be compromised.

Ouzo A strong alcohol that is heavily flavoured with anise. Other flavourings come from spices such as cardamom, star anise seed, coriander and lime flowers. Every region of Greece creates their own version of Ouzo. A good bottle of ouzo can be easily found at your local liquor store.

Roe Eggs from fish such as carp or cod. When these eggs are blended with potatoes and lemon juice it is called "Taramosalata". The colour of the dip can range from creamy beige to bright pink depending on the type of roe used.

Saganaki Literally means "little frying pan" but today the term is synonymous with a popular appetizer that consists of frying salty cheeses. Cheeses such as Kefalotiri or Kefalograviera are often used and in some restaurants the cheese is also flambéed.

Semolina Semolina is made from hard durum wheat. It can be found coarsely ground or finely ground into flour.

Vanilla powder Simply made by grinding vanilla beans until you get a fine white powder. Vanilla powder can be added to warm liquids and the vanilla flavour will not evaporate as it would when using vanilla extract.

Greek Recipe Index

Index

Index

Thank you

We would like to thank everyone who encouraged us to pursue this project when it was only an idea, an idea that seemed to come at a time in our lives when we couldn't find a reason not to do it. Other than the long days and nights, the difficulty of trying to work with 5 children under 10, the fact that one of us had just had a newborn baby and survived on very little sleep, the fact that each of us lived in a different city, the fact that it was the greyest and wettest summer on record for 100 years, and we relied on the sun for all of our photos, other than all of these challenges, foreseen and not foreseen, we still felt that this was the perfect project at the perfect time.

A special thank you to Jay Ouelette who first encouraged us to pursue this project.

To Diane Alexopoulos for all of your great ideas, and advice, and for opening up endless opportunities for us to consider, thank you.

Thank you to the staff of the The Bookshelf and eBar, for your wonderful support of local authors and for helping us put together our first book launch.

Thank you to Emily Richards and Elizabeth Baird for lending us your ears even though you didn't know who we were.

To Kate and Paul Mlodzik and Paola and Chris Hohenadel for tolerating the tireless conversation about this project over our many get-togethers, thanks for listening.

Thank you to Georges Philippouci for doing a wonderful job printing our book. Thank you for answering every single question we had at all hours of the day. You are a patient man. We are so lucky to have you as part of our family.

Thank you to our good friends Nicole and Garry Round, for helping us along the way, whether it was testing recipes, offering accounting advice, answering computer questions, and for being our biggest fans. Your unwavering belief in the success of this book has been appreciated.

Thank you to our wonderful children who were forced to eat many dishes over and over again until they were perfected. We may have been busier than usual, but we think you will really be grateful one day.

To our hubbies, Jonathan, Sean and Eric: thanks for your faith in this project, and your constant love and support.

Thank you to our parents. Thank you will never, ever be enough.

Printed for

adelfes

Originally published October 2009
Montréal, Québec Canada
Third printing